Strengthen Your Business Process Backbone

Strengthen Your Business Process Backbone

The unappreciated value of facilitating processes

Jeffrey L. Dauphinee

Copyright © 2021 Jeffrey L. Dauphinee. All Rights Reserved.
jeffrey.dauphinee@gmail.com

Print ISBN: 9798554576324
Kindle Direct Publishing, Independent Publishing Platform

Contents

Figures   vii
Introduction   1

Chapter One   5
    "What are your amphipods?"

Chapter Two   13
    "Keep one hand on the tee-handle
    and one foot under the rope."

Chapter Three   21
    "The backbone processes are more proprietary
    than the value stream steps."

Chapter Four   35
    "We saw additional, unanticipated benefits."

Chapter Five   41
    "How do we ever get anything done
    if we keep changing direction?"

Chapter Six   47
    "The new role and process have been proven as effective,
    but the timing is just not right."

Chapter Seven   53
    "Are you playing football or fútbol?"

Chapter Eight   59
    "No number eleven!"

Chapter Nine   67
    "Facilitating process steps were missing."

Chapter Ten   85
    "After more than a decade,
    it was still in place and being constantly improved."

Chapter Eleven   95
    "She was tracking and managing all of this
    in a spreadsheet."

Chapter Twelve   109
    "If they fail, they can have significant impact."

Chapter Thirteen   117
    "What is your No Number Eleven?"

Notes   123
Index   125
Acknowledgments   127
About the Author   129

Figures

Figure 1. Value Stream and Backbone Process Direct Impact — 7

Figure 2. Look for Backbone Processes That Align to Multiple Value Stream Steps — 14

Figure 3. Pareto — 63

Figure 4. Training Value Stream and Facilitating Processes — 69

Figure 5. Competency Profile — 75

Figure 6. Module D2 Loading Product — 75

Figure 7. Training Plan Outline — 75

Figure 8. Average Training Duration — 82

Figure 9. Stakeholder Satisfaction Survey — 87

Figure 10. Trainee Proficiency — 89

Figure 11. Productivity Gain — 91

Figure 12. Inventory of Process Change — 103

Figure 13. Data Elements in a Change Record — 104

Introduction

On Mother's Day I bought a pair of kayaks for my wife and me so that we could enjoy time together on lakes in our area. The first few trips went well, and we explored shorelines that we had never seen before. Then on one of our trips, after we paddled a lake for about three hours we decided to bring the kayaks into shore. As I went to lift one of the kayaks, my back went into an excruciating spasm where my muscles contracted which in turn put intense pressure on nerves that caused pain at a level I have never previously experienced. A man who had observed all of this came over and helped my wife lift me into the passenger side of our Subaru and then put the kayaks on the roof racks. I was taken to an emergency room at a nearby hospital to be treated. After several tests, the physician determined that I needed potassium replacement and prescribed muscle relaxant medication. When your back is in pain, your entire body is affected and so even the most mundane daily tasks like walking and sitting are difficult to perform. It took a week to recover and there was minor residual discomfort for months.

What was the cause? Evidently dehydration and a diet deficient in potassium led to muscle cramps and spasms. What appears to be an acute event is more often a series of issues that build over time. During my recovery, daily stretches and adjustments to my diet improved the condition of my muscles. I was fortunate because some people have more structural and anatomical issues leading to chronic symptoms and which can require surgery or other demanding treatments.

I relate this story to demonstrate that less visible processes can have substantial impact on our health. This occurs in business systems just as it does in our human body. Critical but unappreciated factors affect daily operations. Sometimes—like my back spasm—failures are a one-time acute issue. Other times, they are chronic problems that we attempt to solve again and again without success.

You may have experienced something similar in your own work, where you have failed multiple times at trying to correct a systemic problem. This type of scene is common across all segments and at all levels of organizations. There are thorny problems that we do not solve—at least not for long. Teams that I have worked with and led have discovered and applied an effective practice to diagnose and treat these types of failure modes.

The journey, the results, the insights, and the solutions will enable anyone to improve their ability to identify significant causes and implement effective, sustainable, and flexible improvements. Gaining appreciation for what we refer to as backbone business processes is a key to your success.

How the Book Is Organized

Chapters one and two include a detailed description of backbone processes and consider common questions and arguments raised about them. In chapters three and four, you will read about mortgage originations where we found deficiencies in both the value stream and the backbone. Using this as our first example will illustrate not only the vital nature of the supporting process, but also how the value stream and backbone interact. I include the set of actions typically taken in analyzing and strengthening your foundational activities. The mortgage sales and fulfillment organization faced a dynamic and competitive environment as well as vigorous regulatory oversight. It needed to be flexible and responsive to the rapid pace of change. I use this experience to demonstrate an insight which continues to positively influence my design work in a variety of other applications.

Chapters five, six, and seven describe applying these practices in a call center, small business banking, and a local residential flooring installation company. In chapters eight through eleven, I provide a deep dive into two large scale facilitating processes—employee training and change management. These two cases are valuable on two levels. First, they show the depth of our work and the results. Second, they may be directly valuable in your organization because both training and change management are fundamental in nearly every business. Additionally, both of these workflows are large enough to within themselves have components of value stream and supporting activities.

In chapters twelve and thirteen I share thoughts about applying the analysis of value stream and facilitating processes to several different types of industry applications, and then wrap up with a summary and instructions on how you can use what you have learned.

Drawing from the challenges and successes in these different settings, you will read interesting stories of diagnosing causes and our approach to developing solutions, but more important than the specific examples are the lessons learned and insights gained. In doing this work, the teams learned the vital role of the business process backbone. We were also influenced by the Project Management Institute's "A Guide to the Project Management Body of Knowledge,"[1] the "Capability Maturity Model Integration"[2] developed by Carnegie Innovations, quality management, and process design methodologies.[3] This is not to say that our project work fully implemented these disciplines, but rather that we borrowed concepts which enabled our success. It is not my intent to go into detail on these areas of expertise and methods but to reference them and what was borrowed from them as we approached the work being described. The ongoing application of these and other methodologies toward better design with the correct balance of repeatability and flexibility continues to be my main pursuit.

You may wish to select some of what is covered in this book while skipping other elements of our practices. I do offer a basic structure you can use, but it is not meant to convey a strict set of steps. This series of discoveries is intended to assist you in your efforts to resolve and avoid deeply rooted and challenging failures. There are many effective root-cause analysis, problem solving, continuous improvement, and corrective action frameworks offered by other authors. My contribution is not another framework but is to bring additional perspective and make whichever method you choose to use more effective.

Chapter One

"What are your amphipods?"

In the introduction I described my experience with an intense muscle spasm in my back and how I relate my treatment to foundational failures in an enterprise. That injury affected every move I made and changed all aspects of daily life until the treatment, dietary changes, and daily stretches healed and strengthened my muscles. Similarly, failures or weakness in business backbone processes can affect your daily operations. Here in chapter one, I introduce the definitions of the value stream and backbone and how they interrelate. This understanding came through the result of unsuccessful experience and our subsequent research which led to multiple sustained successes.

Value Stream and Facilitating Processes

In the Project Management Institute 2000 edition of the Guide to the Project Management Body of Knowledge ("PMBOK") descriptions of "core" and "facilitating" processes were defined in section 3.3.2. Core processes have planning dependencies that require them to be completed in the same sequence on most projects. Facilitating processes are different because they are performed intermittently throughout the project rather than in a specific order.

This concept of core and facilitating operations became a key insight and point of discussion for the engineering teams that I have led. As we debated the implications of this intriguing concept, we arrived at a method for applying it. Our definitions proved to be instrumental to success. My teams have applied them to a diverse set of cases in financial services, manufacturing, small business, and non-profit organizations. They span across mortgage originations, call center customer service, small business banking services, change management, training, and a residential renovation venture. Based on my experience, I believe they can apply to your interest as well.

CORE or VALUE STREAM: A key activity or cluster of activities which must be performed in an exemplary manner to ensure a firm's continued competitiveness because it adds primary value to an output.[4]

FACILITATING or BACKBONE: An activity or cluster of activities that do not of themselves add primary value to a customer or end-user output but are performed internally by the organization to make it possible to accomplish the core business. These supporting functions often relate to multiple value stream steps.[5]

In the remainder of this book, I will commonly refer to the core processes as the value stream in a clear reference to adding value for the customer or end user.

I heard one chief operating officer of a Fortune 25 corporation refer to facilitating activities as "backbone processes" so I have adopted that term and will use it interchangeably with terms like facilitating, enabling, supporting, and foundational as I believe that these descriptions are effective in conveying the concept.

The value stream requires agility and flexibility, but the backbone tends to be stable for a long period of time.

Value stream steps are those that most directly impact the customer. In health care the value stream includes scheduling an appointment, conducting medical examinations and tests, providing the results, discussing treatment options with the patient, implementing the treatment, and arranging for payment.

In contrast, the backbone is more internally focused and, although necessary, does not directly or immediately impact the customer. Insurance billing is a facilitating function at health care providers. Patients really do not care to get involved in how the medical office bills the insurance carrier, but they do expect the billing to be accurate and they want to be informed of how much the insurance paid toward the medical bill. It is noteworthy here to explain that within nearly any business, you could identify value stream and enabling elements. This is a recursive concept, where even within large-scale backbone processes there can be both value stream and foundational activities. More on this later in the chapter. Other enabling functions include safety management, risk management, technology management, change management, and human resource management.

Value stream processes have greater direct impact on customers and backbone processes have a greater direct impact on the associates or team members who are employees of the organization (figure 1).

Figure 1. Value Stream and Backbone Process Direct Impact

Value Stream Process	Backbone Process
Customer	Associate / Team Member
Stakeholder	Stakeholder
Associate / Team Member	Customer

(Greatest Impact ↑)

These internal functions tend to stay more stable and consistent. They are not as commonly impacted by product changes or exogenous effects. They have a foundational role in how the overall business operates and, therefore, the backbone should be bedrock that supports the value stream. The facilitating processes require robust change management governance to enable them to adjust their content to a changing value stream. If properly designed, the fundamentals of supporting structures will not generally need to change frequently. They can be stable enough to be incrementally improved through many years and generations of products or services. In fact, we will see that a competitive advantage and proprietary capability is more often embedded in the backbone.

The value stream depends on the backbone but is heavily impacted by customer demands and by the external environment. Because these changes are not in the control of the enterprise, they drive rapid and unpredictable need for change.

As a metaphor, consider an ocean. The facilitating process is the regular and predictable ocean tide. I can find out exactly when high or low tide will occur at a given beach, even months in advance. I will not likely predict the height of the tide until much closer to the date and time, but I do at least know when it will happen. On top of this regular rhythmic pattern, millions of waves swell and dissipate at unpredictable magnitude and periodicity.

These ocean waves are like the value stream which reacts to a multitude of subtle as well as extreme temperature differences, shifting winds, and storms. The tidal movement forms the foundation and then the individual waves seem to ride on top and are free to modulate based on ever changing conditions. Our challenge is to construct the structures which in turn enable the constantly evolving value stream to modulate as needed.

Think about these illustrations of value stream and backbone processes:

- The air traffic control infrastructure which facilitates the specific flight you take on a trip.
- The stable system of highways and driving laws as enabling the value stream of driving a car anywhere you wish.
- A network of cell phone towers and satellites supports data and voice communications.
- Long held corporate ethics and values that shoulder business goals which can change from year to year.
- Principles and fundamental truths which empower belief and behavior.
- Project management and agile development which facilitate improvement in an enterprise.

Large-Scale Facilitating Processes

Earlier, I mentioned that some supporting operations are large enough to have their own value stream and facilitating components. This is a recursive concept where the repeated definition is applied again at the lower-level sub-process. Let us take air traffic control that enables thousands of flights to many destinations every day. Within air traffic control, we can understandably define a sub-set of value stream steps with pilots as the customers. And the sub-set of backbone functions could include the technology, staffing, training, and regulations.

A highway system facilitates travel and transportation, but given the size and complexity, it has both value stream and foundational components. It includes the roads, entrances, exits, bridges, overpasses, lighting, signage, safety features, and speed limits. These are enabling processes. Then there are the vehicles that use the highway including cars, trucks, motorcycles, and buses. They represent the value stream where customers (passengers and freight) move from one place to another. You can easily imagine that while some failures occur directly because of driver or vehicle issues (value stream), others can be caused by failure of the infrastructure (supporting, backbone) such as rough pavement, weakened bridges, floods, and wind damage.

The massive network of cell phone towers and satellite transceivers across the world enable connectivity of people through technology. The value stream is the communication of data and voice across the combination of radio waves and cables and brings the streaming of a video source to millions of mobile phone customers. The facilitating activities include tower installations, the necessary equipment maintenance, and an ever-growing set of applications that enable mobile phones to access social media, video streaming, make purchases, financial services, transportation, and even making phone calls. Here again, while some failures exist due to a person not responding to a message (value stream), other failures can occur due to infrastructure (backbone) including poor signal strength, cell tower power outages, and your device running out of battery life.

To determine when a facilitating structure is large enough to warrant break down into its own value stream and supporting sub-processes, I offer this guidance. Watch for instances where one or more of the following is true of your business backbone functions:

- Multiple groups or teams are required.
- Significant failure modes exist, often related to more than one part of the value stream.
- You have identified unacceptable risks, quality defects, or expense.
- Variability and confusion abound.
- You have tried multiple times without success to improve a defect or failure mode.

In any of these cases, I suggest deconstructing the large-scale foundational activities into their own value stream and facilitating elements. This is fundamental to establishing a robust and sustainable solution to enable your desired value stream performance and flexibility.

Keystone Species

I often look to nature for inspiration on how to understand my work. An interesting phenomenon has been discovered known as keystone species. In a natural environment there are what we might think of as value stream species which are the ones we readily observe. Behind the scenes, there are facilitating species that enable the ecosystem for the value stream. Amphipods are a keystone species within the ocean.[6] While ubiquitous, they are small and generally unseen, but they are absolutely critical. There are thousands of types of amphipods, and they have a common trait as being near the bottom of the food chain. They begin a domino effect upon which successively larger animals depend through a food web. If something were to endanger amphipods it would erode the entire biological landscape. This is how facilitating processes work in support of a value stream. If they are broken, the impacts show up all through the value stream, but the root cause is not in the value stream—it is most often hidden in the backbone practices.

They exist across the broad scale of size as well. Whether you work at a large corporation, a small business, a local non-profit, or in government administration. The amount of effort will vary across the continuum of scale based on resources and the magnitude of the impact due to a failure mode in one of these supportive activities.

In a simpler, less complex setting like a small business or a small office, use an "and" approach. To improve onboarding and training you could ask a new person coming in to your team to document their training experience for subsequent people going through the same onboarding and training. In another illustration, to improve your supply chain management directly ask your suppliers to share what other small businesses or small offices are doing that appear to be creative solutions which could apply to you. This "and" approach can lead you to identify solutions to the current failure modes in your facilitating processes while you are completing your daily work.

The objective is to identify "your amphipods" and from there, you can focus on design and improvement. There are many effective methods, and you can decide on what method works best in your situation. Selection factors include complexity, required skills, management buy-in, scale of your operations, and available resources.

The important point that I am making is to understand that these enabling processes are critical but often unappreciated in terms of the impact to you and to your customers. As you read through our experiences, use the elements that fit your situation and skip over others that are not well suited for your current need. Some additional ideas are given in chapter twelve.

Chapter One Summary

- Definitions of value stream and backbone processes
- The impact relationship to customers, stakeholders, and internal team members
- What are your "amphipods?"

Chapter Two

"Keep one hand on the tee-handle and one foot under the rope."

What about Being Lean and Agile?

Doesn't a lean organization try to eliminate non-value add steps as waste?

Lean methodology separates activities into value add or non-value add. In real practice, it is not as simple as those two categories and so we hear terms like business value add or necessary non-value add to address work that falls somewhere between the two. In a manufacturing assembly line, parts need to arrive at just the right time to avoid inventory waste, but the supply chain management to get the right parts to arrive at just the right time is not, strictly speaking, adding value, though it is essential in the production effort. My argument goes further in stating that in some cases, these supporting tasks can lead to greater success in the value stream. The question, of course, is which of them to enhance and which of them to minimize because they are considered as waste.

Applying the non-value add test to all of your work is an important venture. When done with an understanding of the essential contribution from backbone processes, you can identify the 20 percent of enablers leveraged by 80 percent of your goods or services.

How do I decide which supporting activities have value?

A manager that I once worked for had a sticky note on his computer monitor in his office. It had two questions on it. "What am I working on?" "What should I be working on?" He was reminding himself that only a portion of the work we do yields results. The rest may have some level of importance, but it does not lead to effective output. The same is true of the enabling functions—only a few make a big difference.

To determine where to invest, consider activities that enable multiple value stream steps as depicted in figure 2.

Figure 2. Look for Backbone Processes that align to Multiple Value Stream Steps

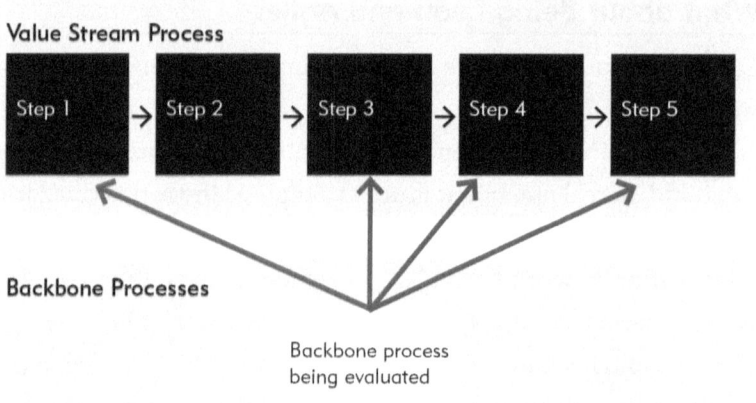

Further analysis can reveal which supporting processes relate to your common failure modes, customer complaints, risks, and innovating opportunities. Base this evaluation on factors like your goals and objectives, customer experience, success metrics, expense, cycle time, defects, rework, pull-through, and fall out. As I related in the introduction, I had to learn the causes of my back spasm and how to prevent them in the future. If I had understood this prior to my spasm,

I could have done some simple things to avoid it. I took my large muscles for granted but when they failed, it caused severe pain and disrupted my normal lifestyle for weeks. It affected every movement I tried to make, small or large. If you have already experienced defects, errors, and failures, there are reactive methods to investigate them and determine solutions. If you wish to avoid failures or you are designing a business and are forward looking, you can add significant advantage through a healthy and strong backbone. Use a risk and opportunity perspective to prevent failure modes and optimize the strength of your value proposition. In chapter three I describe both reactive root-cause analysis and a proactive approach through risk assessment.

In a medical office, the discussion of treatment plans with the patient, determining insurance coverage of the recommended plans and the direct treatment of patients are all in the value stream. They tend to impact the customer (in this case the patient) more than they impact the shareholders and the associates working in the office. In this same medical office, the training of staff, the internal routing of patient data between scheduling and billing systems, and the transcription of physician's visit notes from an audio recording to written notes for the patient's file are facilitating processes and tend to impact the associates working in the medical office more than they impact the shareholders and the patients who are the customers of the office.

A significant difference between value stream and enabling activities is that value stream steps need to be flexible to meet customer needs and external environmental conditions that are constantly changing. As a result, it is often better for the value stream to be more agile and flexible. If you invest a lot of time and effort into making it too rigid, there will be added expense and challenges when facing required changes.

In many projects that I have led, the fundamental requirements and business case for delivering an improvement changed before the project work could be completed and the new design implemented. This drove rework and a great deal of confusion for the project team, leading to frustration, wasted effort, and expense. In my initial thinking, I would fight against this by trying to sell the senior management team on the need for a robust and stable value stream. After many such experiences, I began to question the rationale of why that was good. The breakthrough came as I more carefully studied the inherent differences between the value stream and the facilitating process.

It was a moment of enlightenment as I realized that the value stream steps are ever changing and rapidly evolving. In some situations, they are rarely stable for more than weeks or months. Supporting structures will also change over time, but generally if they are well designed by using more robust techniques such as the PMI knowledge areas, quality management, and the capability maturity model they can last for years—even through some challenging external environments. One key is that robust foundational activities must include formal change control within the solution. Change control will enable the workflow to be modified as needed but will maintain its integrity. Continuous improvement is achieved through a series of repeating tasks through the cycle of plan-do-check-act as described within the context of the Capability Maturity Model Integration in chapter three.

Facilitating processes are more internal and often can remain stable over a longer period. In fact, there is evidence that where these facilitating processes are well defined and established, there is a sustained benefit to the enterprise and shareholders and often to the customer experience. Stable and effective elements such as human resource management, data management, financial management, risk management, supply chain management, and quality control will form an operational backbone that has far reaching benefits, both internal and external.

Clay Christensen in his book "The Innovator's Dilemma"[7] explained that "Some of the most crucial processes to examine as capabilities or disabilities aren't the obvious value-adding processes involved in logistics, development, manufacturing, and customer service. Rather they are the enabling or background processes that support investment decision-making." He warned that these must enable organizations to be flexible and allow change. I believe that it is through well-defined facilitating structures that constant change can be accomplished, but if poorly defined, neglected, or missing, the required change does not have the necessary channel through which to flow. Adaptability and flexibility require well-defined change management.

Whitewater and the Agile Philosophy

On vacation in the state of Maine, I took a whitewater rafting trip down the Kennebec River which has some class-five water. We were required to start with safety training where we were taught how to navigate and stay as safe as possible. Our guide then gave us two basic rules to follow. One, always keep one hand on the tee-handle of your paddle. Two, always keep one of your feet under the rope across the bottom of the whitewater raft. It was an interesting contrast between the expected excitement of whitewater and the simple but constant instructions for our safety.

In a supplemental video, called Whitewater, bundled with Stephen R. Covey's book titled *The 8th Habit*,[8] he relates that "Everything is changing, and not only is it changing but it is changing at an accelerated rate. It's permanent whitewater, it's constant churning, changing environment. So, it necessitates having a response that does not change. I suggest there are only three constants. One is change, two is principles, and three, choice—the power that you and I have to adapt to the other two constants. The greatest need we have in this whitewater world, this permanent whitewater world, is something that does not change. A changeless core. If people have principles at their center, so that it's a changeless core, it gives them the capacity to deal with the dynamic changes that surround them. That's the whole concept of the nature of leadership today, it is that the more you can get people committed to a common vision, a common purpose, a common set of principles, and they already have it inside them, then the leadership work has been done."

What Covey refers to as a constant, common set of principles, can be compared with the idea of stable, facilitating processes. In his analogy of permanent whitewater, you cannot possibly move quickly enough to navigate the turbulence and accelerating change (agility) without simultaneously having something constant (stability) that can be relied upon. Imagine trying to give a set of detailed, step-by-step instructions to a group of whitewater rafters! While it at first seems to be contradictory, it is a set of constants that help you become agile and flexible, but not lose your way. I assert that the enabling activities, if designed and implemented well, do just that. As successful as implementing the agile philosophy of managing change through constant adaptation may be, it could lead to instability and failure if we do not combine it with a stable foundation.

There is a basic pattern learned through our work. Most of this should be familiar, but the additional focus on the business process backbone presents the significant opportunity.

1. Write out your value stream steps.

    Think about starting with your customer and ending with your customer and where they see value.

2. Write out your backbone activities.

    List the other work that you do which is not visible to your customer. These tend to be internal operations. Consider that some may be missing as you will see in our mortgage example.

3. Assess the value of each activity and function.

    You can use three ratings; customer value-add, internal business value-add, non-value add which is also known as waste.

4. Conduct root-cause analysis as a reactive method.

   For known failure modes, you can use a root-cause analysis method to find why the defects are occurring.

5. Complete a risk and opportunity assessment as a proactive method.

   The most effective technique is to intentionally design facilitating processes to achieve the strongest possible value-add.

6. Prioritize the most critical ones for investment to create your competitive and proprietary advantage.

   Define your primary objectives, success metrics, defects, risks, and innovative opportunities. Rate these and use the rating to identify the most critical area.

7. Design the backbone functions.

   Use the structure of common features and operational framework shared in chapter three.

8. Pilot and test.

9. Use the initial outcome and learning to refine.

10. Implement and measure your results.

    These actions will be demonstrated in greater detail for the mortgage originations case.

Lean organizations often remove or minimize investment in the supporting functions, but we have learned from our experience that when carefully selected, the right foundation ensures a better product or service for the customer.

There are times in leadership when we make critical decisions about where to invest. Times when we need to commit to real fundamental change which takes longer, but which also endures longer. The upcoming case studies were possible because leaders made the investment and did not back down when we faced the inevitable challenges. You will see that some took two or more years, but others were surprisingly quick. The full commitment of leadership makes the difference in being successful.

Chapter Two Summary

- Analyze your backbone functions for value
- Evaluate flexibility vs. stability
- Navigate constant whitewater
- Follow the recommended approach to strengthen your business process backbone

Chapter Three

"The backbone processes are more proprietary than the value stream steps."

Mortgage—Part 1

In this first example, I describe our experience at a U.S. mortgage lender facing competition from both large bank lenders as well as non-bank entities who lend but do not receive deposits. These non-bank mortgage originators tended to offer better technology and customer experience. Senior executives formed a team to reduce the time it takes for customers to obtain a loan to refinance an existing mortgage or purchase a new property. The team first concentrated on documenting the current state. After numerous site visits, focus group sessions, side-by-side sessions, walking the process, and reviewing success metrics, the team found unacceptable variation throughout the sales and fulfillment operations. For some tasks, multiple roles could do them depending on who got to it first. In others, no one seemed to lay claim for being responsible. Even though thousands of customers were getting a funded loan, the procedures were not well defined and there was internal competition that rewarded teams who out-performed other teams. This incented more variation because if you were stack-ranked toward the top, you did not want to share your practices. One of the leaders on this effort returned and stated, "We could not document the current state because no two people could describe it the same way."

Due to the variation, when changes were introduced they were not really implementing one change because the process was not the same in each location or team. If the steps are not consistently understood, the change being implemented looks different to everyone. But if you have a consistent baseline, then each update can be implemented with one effort across the enterprise. It is challenging enough to introduce change without having an uneven foundation on which to build.

Antonio, the senior executive, assigned the business process design team to achieve greater consistency, underwrite applications much more quickly, and improve the customer experience.

When executives make this kind of assignment, it is usually accompanied by a nearly impossible timeframe to complete the work. A healthy tension from an aggressive schedule can be good, but if you want a sustainable correction for fundamental flaws it will take time. We confirmed with Antonio that the highest priority was getting it right.

There are basic, high level operations that most can agree to, but beyond that there was too much variation. When the current process is not well defined and no two people can agree on the exact sequence of activities, it requires something closer to a whiteboard approach where the team needs to define what the target state should be. We followed seven actions to develop the new design.

Action One:
List the value stream in sequential order

The team defined the value stream steps which include major milestones.

1.0 Take an application

2.0 Provide disclosures to the borrower

3.0 Obtain documented evidence of income, assets, and liabilities

4.0 Make a borrower credit risk decision

5.0 Obtain documented evidence of property value and condition, insurance, and property title

6.0 Make a final loan approval decision

7.0 Prepare closing disclosures and documents

8.0 Close and fund the mortgage

Each of these milestones must contain multiple activities with clearly defined roles and responsibilities, inputs and outputs, performance metrics, and controls. There is a combination of science and art in mapping out the workflow. We identified 90 steps that could occur between the first customer contact and a closed, funded loan. In any process flow, handoffs and decisions deserve additional attention as these lead to higher risk and defects. They are also where there is the greatest likelihood of delays. The number of days between the first customer contact and the funded loan was our primary success metric.

I asked one of our engineers to analyze the data and generate a view of the application moving through the life cycle as if we attached a camera to the application. It took several months to join the data tables and fields required to make this view a reality. In lean, this is known as the activity of the product—in this case, the loan application. When the engineer completed the views, it was a breakthrough in our understanding. Instead of a small handful of people touching the application with a few handoffs, we found that dozens of team members and handoffs were occurring. I do not think that anyone on the management team could have predicted the complexity that we discovered. It allowed us to redraw the reality of the current state flow.

During the time that our engineer was creating the handoff views, we focused on the supporting processes.

Action Two:
List the backbone business processes

As described in chapter one, backbone activities enable the value stream and are fundamental to its success.

Facilitating processes include:

1.0 Manage third party relationships

These include the ability to get title insurance, homeowners hazard insurance, property appraisal value, and settlement agent services.

2.0 Set credit policy

Established with consideration to the risk appetite, investor guidance, regulatory requirements, and other similar factors.

3.0 Determine pricing

Influenced by the federal reserve federal funds rate, treasury bond yields, current application volume, and other such determinants.

4.0 Delegate lending authority

A type of certification or internal licensing activity, which ensures governance of who can make underwriting decisions to approve or deny loan applications.

5.0 Plan mortgage team capacity

In coordination with the finance team, calculate the staffing required by role for the forecasted application volume.

There are numerous other foundational efforts including managing human resources, compensation, legal matters, compliance, risk, projects, technology, and on and on. In chapter thirteen I will provide a more comprehensive list.

In this case, we discovered that several facilitating operations were well designed and implemented. There was room for improvement, but they were effectively supporting the value stream process. This is due to being in a highly regulated business sector where mature designs ensure compliance. However, capacity planning for staffing the production team was not effective. This demonstrates that you may identify missing or extremely weak enabling systems. These can be break-through discoveries that lead to impressive performance improvement.

In addition to defining a capacity planning methodology, we prioritized defining a baseline for the value stream. The team made a substantial reset in terms of the objectives and timeline to develop and test from sales through fulfillment and to a funded loan. It obviously borrowed heavily from what was in place, but clearer definitions were needed for each role and responsibility. Inputs and outputs were established for each step. Consistent service level agreements were established to ensure more stability in the expected cycle time of each milestone phase and to improve timeline predictability for borrowers. When customers did not respond within the required timeline, more effective communications were implemented to negotiate and understand the acceptable timeline. Additional metrics were added to manage and control critical inputs.

Action Three:
Perform root-cause analysis

If you know of current errors, defects, complaints, or failure modes, then the reactive methods are effective in diagnosing the causes.

We conducted root cause analysis using standard tools and methods which included the five-whys coupled with Ishikawa fish bone diagramming. The common practices for these methods generally use a set of topics like people, process, procedure, tools, materials, environment, and management. These are intended to guide the team toward various causes for a stated problem. The one significant modification that we made was to include facilitating processes in these topics. This is a critical success factor! The root cause analysis diagrams are written as potential defects such as the lack of something working correctly. In our specific instance we included the lack of production team capacity planning in our Ishikawa diagram. Most people who have conducted root cause analysis would agree that it requires the application of both science and art. The science is the structure and analytical portion, and the art is the creative thinking portion. It is not my intent to describe the entire root cause analysis methodology since there are excellent sources available for this information.

Before embarking on this kind of effort, it is wise to be careful with how you define your problem. An interesting reference on this topic is the book "what's your problem?" written by Thomas Wedell-Wedellsborg[9] in which he shares some great ways to frame a problem. Using different frames may lead to far simpler solutions. If not, it will confirm that you have correctly defined the problem before you invest substantial time into developing solutions.

It is direction first, then velocity![10] If you do not go deep enough, you may move quickly but not solve the real problem. This is an important consideration especially for agile scrum teams because it is crucial to first define the objective. We often herald a sense of urgency—and that is good so long as you first have clarity of purpose.

In my experience with root cause analysis, I find that it is iterative. You might have a working session that leads to a certain set of causes. As you evaluate those causes, you decide that you need another working session to go deeper to reach the systemic failure modes. We found that we needed people from a variety of experience levels, perspectives, disciplines (engineering, production, management, quality), and an experienced facilitator to guide the sessions.

One of my favorite observations is seeing a root cause theme show up in multiple branches of the analysis. These common themes indicate a failure mode that is likely related to a facilitating process and could be significant in getting to a breakthrough. These points are also where the art of root cause analysis is essential in being open minded to completely different ways of thinking about the problem.

Understanding the true underlying cause takes some effort, but if you do not make the effort to get all the way there, you will not address the right failure mode.

Action Four:
Conduct a risk and opportunity assessment

You may be wondering if we always have to be reactive to an existing problem. No!

One effective method for analyzing your process to identify potential failure modes and breakthrough opportunities is to complete a risk and opportunity assessment. There are many excellent references for risk assessments, so I will just offer a brief description here for you to envision how this could be applied to your situation.

- First, write down the value stream process steps. Think about your customer and what you do that directly delivers value to them.

- For each value stream step, list the possible failure modes and errors that can take place. Give special attention to decision points and handoffs from one person to another. These decisions and handoffs represent significant risk.

- Then for each of these failure modes or errors, rate them in terms of how significant the failure would be for you and your customer.

- Next, rate each failure mode for how likely it is to occur.

- And then, rate each failure mode for how quickly you would know if the failure or error had occurred.

- From these ratings, rank your risks in order of greatest risk to lowest risk by their impacts.

- With this ranking, you can decide which risks you need to mitigate and that are worth your investment.

Assessing risks and considering mitigation options can lead you to proprietary and competitive advantages like the examples I will share below and also in chapter seven where you will read about how a small business effectively used a proactive risk assessment to avoid costly mistakes.

In chapter twelve, you will see some ideas from a variety of industries and applications to identify facilitating processes which could be valuable for you to implement.

As you move toward solutions, innovative ideas should be assessed instead of simply a repair-and-fix kind of approach. This is where an agile philosophy can lead you to creative new ways to remove the root cause failure mode and to mitigate anticipated risks. You can increase your velocity toward a solution.

In the mortgage originations improvement project, we did not have anything specifically pointing us to the lack of capacity planning. In previous designs and with experience in other sectors like manufacturing, knowing the required number of resources was required. That experience led us to question the current planning process which seemed to be inadequate—nearly non-existent. Therefore, in addition to adding capacity planning to our root cause analysis, we took a more proactive tack and included it in a comprehensive risk assessment. A really interesting factor emerges when considering capacity planning. It is the interaction between the value stream and the backbone functions. The capacity plan had to represent the work required in the value stream workflow, so the value stream process was built out and implemented before we could set the values needed to calculate capacity requirements. It is not uncommon for this kind of interaction and iteration to take place between value stream and facilitating processes. It requires testing.

In our piloting and testing, we conducted time studies to understand exactly how much work the steps took. We temporarily pulled a portion of the staff off the production team and assigned them to cross-training and other activities so that we could validate the level of staffing we left in production. We effectively lowered the staffing to our theoretical number and through this exercise, we learned the true production capacity and included these values in our capacity planning model. We created a staffing model with our values and validated this with our finance partners. Capacity planning is a competitive advantage for expense management that is an input to the pricing process.

Action Five:
Define your competitive and proprietary advantage

I want to emphasize an important point about these specific facilitating processes—which is that they are more proprietary than the value stream. It is true that lenders can differentiate their products and services in the value stream, but the greatest leverage is in these types of support functions. Loan underwriters assimilate all of the credit and collateral information and decide whether the customer and the property justify the risk of lending money. The decision is made within the value stream, but the guidance for how to make the decision, the parameters of acceptable risk, the algorithms for various financial factors, and the pricing of the loan are all established in the backbone business capabilities that are never seen by the customer. Yet, the underwriting decision is the most important step in the entire end-to-end experience. This is where competitive and proprietary advantage can be leveraged.

As another example, think about the interactions between the lender and the customer. Whether these are through digital applications, chat, email, by phone, or in some cases in person, the manner in which these are conducted and how clear and understandable they are is all empowered behind the scenes by scripting, training, and selection of customer-facing team members. These make-or-break characteristics are what customers talk about when they describe their experience to their family and friends. Time and again, we saw that even if a closing date selected by the customer was moved due to delays, the customer would still rate the experience as satisfactory if the lender communicated clearly and frequently to keep the customer apprised of the reason for the delay and how they could work together to set a new closing date.

Illustrations of proprietary advantage through innovative enabling functions include logistics and fulfillment management technology at online retailers, subscription and personalized recommendation management at entertainment streaming services, and video technology and hosting at online gaming sites.

It is easy to see the significant influence these facilitating processes have on the end-to-end lending operations. Through them, the lender governs its competitive advantage in pricing, credit policy, and underwriting decisions. Additionally, supporting processes are more effective in managing customer experience and risk.

Action Six:
Design effective business processes

Process design is an entire body of knowledge in itself, but to give just a brief insight, we used two constructs from the Capability Maturity Model Integration to guide our development of the mortgage workflow.

The first construct is referred to as the Common Features. Similar to a plan, do, check, act cycle, we used this as the guide to a continuous improvement process and it includes five elements:

- Commitment to Perform
- Ability to Perform
- Activities Performed
- Measurement and Analysis
- Verifying Implementation

The second construct is referred to as the Operational Framework and includes:

- Policies
- Standards
- Process
- Procedures
- Training
- Tools

By integrating these two constructs, we used them in designing the end-to-end mortgage sales and fulfillment activities:

Step 1. Define the commitment to perform the process.

Commitment consists of strategy, policies (laws and regulations that govern or constrain operations), and incentives that motivate the organization to follow the procedures. This commitment should enable individuals to achieve their personal goals while meeting the customer requirements and achieving the organization's goals.

Step 2. Define the ability to perform the process.

This requires standards (acceptance criteria), training (required knowledge and skills), and tools (technology and automated support).

Step 3. Define the activities performed in the process.

Describe "what" happens within the organization to build products and provide services that conform to the standards in accordance with the strategy, values, and policies of the organization. We think of this as the high-level design. The procedures describe "how-to" instructions that implement the process. This is the low-level design and includes the detailed step-by-step direction.

Step 4. Define the measurement and analysis to monitor and control the process.

A control plan describes the control points that are measured to enable the process owner to regularly check the health of operations. The measurement plan defines the metrics that are captured and reported to implement the control plan. Analysis on any given metric leads you to better understand the cause-and-effect relationships and behavior of the process and illuminates where changes may be prioritized and made. Tools such as statistical software and control charts are required to provide performance measurement and analyses.

Step 5. Define the method for verifying implementation of the process.

Having a third party regularly validate execution against the policies and standards keeps the process owner honest and allows for additional insight to be offered.

These five steps apply to the value stream and supportive activities.

To engage stakeholders, we listed nearly one hundred partners who had interest. These included business leaders, finance, technology, risk, compliance, legal, customer experience, quality, human resource, compensation, training, and reporting. Every two weeks we met with a small group of stakeholders and then at least monthly, we met with the entire list of stakeholders. This proved to be essential to our success. You might not think of this as a facilitating process, and in some ways it is not, but through these stakeholder reviews we uncovered issues and failure modes that would have disrupted the workflow had we not addressed them. In fact, these diverse stakeholders most often identified opportunities in the backbone processes.

Action Seven:
Conduct a pilot of your design

I strongly advocate for testing the process changes before implementing them across your entire organization. It is better to learn first in a small, manageable team and then refine based on the results. It also enables you to better describe the changes when you implement them more broadly. You can think of this being consistent with the agile philosophy of develop, test, and learn in a series of sprints. We learned many valuable lessons from our tests which we folded back into development and retesting.

Antonio and other leaders were anxious to see progress, so the team tested and implemented the process in segments. The first segment designed and tested was from taking an application through to the credit risk decision. While this was in test, the team worked on the second segment which then went into a test period. With each successive segment, learning and feedback was used to refine and further improve the workflow. Many questions arose from the frontline team members and managers, so these were captured, answered, and incorporated into the implementation and training plan. We discovered that team member questions were mostly about the baseline process, not our new improvements. This revealed that even production staff with significant tenure had questions about how to do their jobs. The pilot structure gave them a safe condition in which to ask their questions without feeling embarrassment—yet another benefit from this work.

Chapter Three Summary

- A mortgage sales and fulfillment operations example
- Follow the seven actions to analyze and strengthen your business process backbone
- Consider applying the CMMI common features and operational framework in your design
- Create proprietary advantage!

Chapter Four

"We saw additional, unanticipated benefits."

Mortgage—Part 2

The piloting and implementation of the enhanced process was an iterative effort where we tested, learned, improved, and tested again.

It was a major challenge to gain consistent adherence, especially where people applied human judgment. Underwriters decide whether an applicant is a credit worthy risk and whether the property collateral is enough to protect the lender in the event of a mortgage default. This is the most critical decision throughout the process and yet, how do you consistently apply criteria and policy through human judgment? The facilitating functions behind these decisions include the delegation of lending authority to underwriters—provided through advanced training and certification where completed test cases are evaluated by the lending authority team. There is automated decisioning for simpler applications and properties, and use of machine intelligence in moderate cases, but with more complex transactions and properties it still depends on a level of human decision.

To support front-line managers, we wrote a manager playbook that contained the definitive list of reporting and production management tools. Managers received step-by-step instructions for daily routines and gained visibility to all work in their respective areas. Prioritization algorithms guided which applications to work next, and escalation paths allowed management of exceptions. The natural tension between sales and fulfillment is a constant challenge. Every loan officer in sales wants their applications prioritized. Every production team member in fulfillment is caught between the loudest sales voice, their direct manager's voice, and the customer. Not all of this tension was resolved but using a consistent set of queue management calculations can aid in cooperation and ensure that the customer's interest guides all decisions.

Our work confirmed that it takes eighteen months to three years to affect transformational change across an organization's culture to move from one level of maturity to another.[11] Note that in 1919 Frederick Winslow Taylor[12] wrote, "The writer has over and over again warned those who contemplated making this change that it was a matter, even in a simple establishment, of from two to three years, and that in some cases it requires from four to five years." There is something organic and human about how people adapt to change that has not been altered in more than 100 years since Taylor's work at Bethlehem Steel in the early twentieth century! It does not appear to respond to technology or methods, but just takes time and experience. It also includes the full distribution of early adopters, majority adopters, and late adopters. In Taylor's work, he found that when between 25 percent and 33 percent of the staff adapted to a change, there was a tipping point and the change accelerated throughout the organization from that point on. Similarly, David N. Weidman, former CEO of Celanese, a global chemical production corporation, observed that it takes the square root of the number of people in your business to act as change agents and lead the revolution.[13]

For an organization of 1,000 people, Weidman's approach takes the square root of the population, which is 32 people, to act as change agents. Then these 32 need to influence and recruit Taylor's estimate of 25 percent to 33 percent of the population, about 300 people, to achieve the tipping point toward accelerated adoption.

An agile philosophy favors constant, incremental change, but transformational change takes much longer.

After piloting the entire sales and fulfillment process, results included proving capability to achieve desired reduction in the number of days to take an application through to funding, increased customer satisfaction, increased team member satisfaction, and significant improvement in productivity which in turn lowered the cost per loan—a key financial metric.

The senior executive, Antonio, had stated the objectives as achieving operational consistency, to process applications in fewer days, and improve customer satisfaction.

There was loudly voiced frustration from senior leaders for the amount of time taken to do the work. Mid-level leaders had to constantly reassure senior management that the robust approach we took would ultimately pay off and offer a more sustainable set of solutions. To their credit, we were able to conduct the analysis and design work.

How did we do?

The number of calendar days to fund a loan application was reduced by 27 percent, proving strong competitive capability.

Overall customer satisfaction improved slightly by 3 percent, but when we looked at the specific customer metric for "closed the loan on the customer's desired date," it improved by more than 10 percent.

The cost per loan is a financial metric that sums all of the expense incurred to take an application through to funding. This metric was improved by nearly 16 percent, an enormous lever to improve both pricing and profitability.

As with every one of my experiences improving the fundamental supporting processes, we saw additional, unanticipated benefits.

Whether internal improvements and innovation or those driven by external changes such as regulatory requirements and competitive forces, they were now implemented onto a firm, common foundation. This reinforced the consistency that is critical in a heavily regulated financial services enterprise.

We implemented a simple taxonomy and numbered all of the steps. While the activities do not always flow in a linear path, the taxonomy allowed us to directly tie together each step with the related role, procedures, training, policy, controls, and regulatory rules.

Investors, auditors, and regulators now saw a clearly defined and documented process when they asked questions about our practices. Internally, we were all able to talk about the end-to-end lifecycle with common understanding.

We defined guidance for issue escalation and resolution that quieted the noise of ad hoc debates around priorities and unique customer circumstances.

Team member work was prioritized. Two of the most important questions they need to answer are: (1) what work is waiting for me? and (2) of the work that is waiting for me, which is the most important to do next? Answering these two questions enables the flow of loan applications in an optimal order for the business and the customers.

In the initial walkthrough with the production team members, we conducted many side-by-sides and made observations about the current state. A striking conclusion was that the environment was one of low trust. Team members constantly checked all of the work that had been performed before the application arrived in their work queue. After the new workflow rolled out, we saw increased trust across the organization and efficiency gains through reducing these constant checks of previous work.

Before leaving the description of improving the mortgage operations, let me share a vital lesson learned. The best design still depends on leaders and managers consistently directing the daily work, especially for manual efforts. In our case, we had proven capability to realize substantial gains and it is in the hands of leaders to follow the process. You can build a car that has performance, safety, and comfort features but the driver still has to drive it with care. And, just like self-driving cars, until fully automated, the human factor is always a potential failure mode.

Next, I describe evaluation of facilitating processes in other business settings. Even if none of these matches yours, you may borrow from the ideas to better understand how to identify your own supporting functions.

Chapter Four Summary

- Transformational work takes more time than anticipated and requires sponsorship at senior levels of the organization

- A clearly defined process is an important foundation for introducing ongoing improvement and innovation

- The human factor remains a potential failure mode until you can solve for inconsistency through technology

Chapter Five

*"How do we ever get anything done
if we keep changing direction?"*

Call Center

During an operations review session, a mortgage servicing senior executive charged her team with a 10-percent reduction in call center average handle time. With call time currently at just over 400 seconds, this meant a goal of taking off forty seconds. "I'll free up resources that you need, and we have to move quickly. Can you implement the change in two months?" Diana had been emphasizing the need to reduce handling time all year. Performance plans in her organization had a high priority goal for reduction, but now she was out of patience. She chartered a team to take this as the number one priority and get it done.

One of her senior managers opted to use a lean agile scrum[14] and kaizen approach that would initially make the forty-second reduction in the two-month time frame and then continue from there to reduce handle time further. Two engineers visited U.S. call centers in Jacksonville, Florida, Dallas, Texas, and Lancaster, California to conduct time and quality studies through observations during "side-by-side" sessions. They sat next to the front-line associates and connected into the same phone line so that they could hear both ends of the conversations. They noted how many different applications and screens were used, the amount of time devoted to each part of the call, the ability to reference account data and answer customer questions, and the transfer of calls to other associates to handle customer service requests. This data was compiled and analyzed to define the baseline results and to identify opportunity for improvement. I led the engineering team that studied the activity of the product (in this case, the phone call), activity of the associate, activity of the customer, and activity of the various technology platforms. We learned that associates typically accessed more than twelve different applications during each call. Further we learned that multiple and redundant customer verification steps were used, and that most of the time consumed in each call was due to research required to resolve the customer's questions.

Using this data, we compiled a value stream map and applied lean principles to eliminate waste in the call-center processes. This prepared us for the lean agile sprints.

A one-week kick-off included visits at two call center locations. Rapid idea generation was followed immediately with real-time testing on the call center floor. Associates took drafted instructions that were approved on the spot by the call center manager and asked several call center specialists to use them. Simultaneously, specialists with the test instructions were observed and timed while other specialists using the existing instructions were also timed and observed as a control group for comparison. Based on the feedback, edits were made and approved for further testing cycles.

A total of thirty-three ideas were documented with estimated handle time reduction for each idea. Testing confirmed which changes had merit and led to more accurate estimates of the real savings. Team members rated each proposed change for complexity in terms of how many days it would realistically take to develop and implement. Based on these factors, ideas were either accepted for adoption or determined to be out of scope for this effort.

By the end of the week, the team had narrowed the thirty-three ideas to just three that proved to be effective and would reduce at least forty seconds from the average call handle time. A plan was created to formally update the procedures, edit the call center scripting, and change the related quality control functions within six weeks. The team celebrated their plan and went to work on implementation. These changes would be introduced to only two of the call centers while the remaining centers followed the existing process until executive approval for further adoption was received.

Each week the team met to summarize progress and to resolve issues. The senior executive usually attended these sprint showcase calls and monitored the progress toward implementation. As the final week of implementation approached, a status meeting was held with the senior executive and her direct reports. The team members selected Kristin—a bright and outgoing frontline manager—to present. This would be a good opportunity to introduce her to the senior leaders and executives. She prepared the presentation with a brief statement of the original objective outlined by Diana and then the method used by the team, and finally the results which met the original objective, proven by hypothesis testing that showed statistical difference between the test and control group. The team was eager to share this great news and anticipated that Diana would give them high praise.

Instead, the team members were stunned to learn that the operations senior management team had decided to change the focus of call center performance measurement from average handle time to customer experience. This change in focus was intended to improve customer loyalty and resolve frequent re-routing of calls. "Our goal for the coming year is now focusing on customer satisfaction" explained Diana. "We need to improve our customer survey scores by at least ten points and so this may actually increase the average handle time for our calls."

The lean agile scrum team members glanced around the room to measure each other's reactions. They were astonished and nearly in disbelief. They had anticipated appreciation for their work and now they were being given a completely new direction. "But even though our focus will not be on average handle time, this reduction is still a benefit, right?" asked one of the unit managers on the scrum team. "Of course," responded Diana. "But I need you to begin work right away to improve customer satisfaction, so if that means that we don't get all of your ideas implemented for the reduction in handle time across the sites, that will be acceptable."

None of the team members could recall much of what happened for the rest of the meeting. Something about how the operations management team would be developing a new customer survey and how they would measure customer loyalty across all the relationships and accounts with the bank. What they did remember is how their excitement was crushed by Diana's statement of the new direction and sudden shift in priority. As they left the meeting room and headed for lunch, Kristen voiced the question on everyone's mind, "How do we ever get anything done if we keep changing direction?"

Sitting in the cafeteria at the Lancaster, California site, the team looked out over the Joshua trees in the surrounding high desert area. They discussed the new focus. The idea that made the most important contribution toward reducing average call handling time was coincidentally one that also reduced re-routing of calls. Customers who called in were sometimes transferred to other departments and through a series of transfers would go back to the first department that had taken the call in the beginning. This frustrated customers and eroded confidence that they would get resolution to their mortgage servicing questions.

In fact, during this same time frame a rather funny, but all too real, commercial parodied a call center with a man in Siberia known as "Peggy" who speaks with a Romanian accent and passes the phone around the room until it ends up back with him (Discover Card Campaign 2010).[15] This ad symbolized the truth of some customer experiences.

We mapped the value stream steps which include working the call queues, understanding and answering customer questions, meeting customer requests, and carefully documenting the call. Once again, the root causes of deficiency for not only the original focus of average call handle time, but also of the new focus for customer experience and call quality were in the facilitating processes and so our attention turned to defining them.

When you need to contact a business to get some assistance, what is most important to you? Having options to talk with someone or to simply use a chat or instant message option? To have someone knowledgeable respond quickly and get right to the answer you need? To use a self-serve, automated system to get to the answer?

Meeting these customer needs requires a set of supporting functions that include a sophisticated data and information platform, smart call and chat routing, customer service representatives who possess customer empathy, and the ability to concisely convey the answer to customers in clear, straightforward language. Once we aligned our work to addressing these processes, the result was greater than ten points improvement in customer experience surveys without extending average handle time for calls or online chats.

Additional development included team member selection to identify candidates with customer relationship experience and natural empathy. We improved methods of displaying customer account information to the customer service representatives handling the calls and chats. Advanced keyword search capability and indexing of topics enable quick searches for information. Groundwork was completed for future implementation of artificial intelligence (AI)[16] or application programming interface (API)[17] options to service customer requests.

This call center experience underscores how including the enabling processes in our design work can lead to success even when—maybe especially when—the value stream is changing. Reflecting on the whitewater principles from chapter two, we also see that investing in the facilitating processes is relevant during changing business objectives. We should include them with our work on the value stream. This is the theme of the next few examples.

Chapter Five Summary

- A call center example
- In addition to enabling the value stream process steps to change quickly, effective foundational processes also support flexibility in the business objectives

Chapter Six

"The new role and process have been proven as effective, but the timing is just not right."

Small Business Banking

The president of the commercial banking division of a financial services enterprise decided to form a project team to develop a role focused on small business banking. An extremely talented and experienced executive named Tenicia was selected to lead the effort. Tenicia was a perfect fit to lead this team because she emulated the entrepreneurial spirit of small business customers. She set an aggressive goal of growing the segment revenue by at least 15 percent.

Tenicia selected associates from across a broad functional array including specialists from financial product lines, banking center operations, engineering, learning, procedures, finance, legal, compliance, human resources, and compensation. The team studied the current state of small business banking and decided to add a specialist role to banking centers in key market areas where opportunity was high. The team worked for months to design the role with relationship development, sales, and fulfillment activities. Partnerships were formed with merchant services teams who provided credit and debit card equipment and processing. Banking center managers and market executives offered valuable insight into customer needs and behaviors as well as advice on how to fit the new role into the banking center team environment.

A salary structure and incentive framework were developed and approved. Training and job aids were created.

For nearly one year I worked with the team to pilot the role in the south Florida region, using flagship banking centers to test and improve to a point where it was effective for small businesses and profitable for the bank. During this year, the project team travelled to the Miami area to work with banking center managers, market executives, and banking staff. We observed live interactions between bankers and their customers. The team provided training and collected feedback from everybody involved in the pilot. Baseline data had been collected prior to conducting the pilot, and now actual results showed mixed success compared to the baseline at these same locations. In addition, several comparable banking centers in the same south Florida market were selected where small business bankers were not tested, and we used these centers as a control group.

Although sales significantly increased in the pilot banking centers, the net income at these centers did not offset the sales sufficiently to justify the role. This caused us to reevaluate the design of the sales procedures, practices, and routines.

The value stream steps included: sales lead generation, building relationships, conducting a financial needs assessment, product and service sales, fulfillment, servicing customers, and managing the relationships.

We identified facilitating processes to include: The U.S. Small Business Administration loan services, credit policy, finance acuity, the development of financial products and services, and customer referral services.

We decided to add more emphasis on the enabling activities to our scope of work. Studying the financial needs of entrepreneurs, we learned about the critical nature of cash flow, supply chains, staffing, payroll, and other financial services required for them to succeed. We developed products and services to meet these needs including targeted checking, savings, and investment accounts along with enhanced merchant services technology and mobile banking applications. We added features for payroll and tax accounting. We then developed a playbook for the small business banker so that they could effectively work referrals, evaluate the needs of owners, and offer the right set of solutions.

After months of intense work, they succeeded in a statistically significant improvement in services and a resulting lift in net income to the bank that made the new role and services viable. As the team created an implementation plan, a large-scale rollout to multiple markets across the country was anticipated. A second pilot was started in the Chicago market and within months was also showing significant lift in sales and net income that exceeded the initial goal. Eagerly, Tenicia and her team presented the full rollout plan to senior executives and the division president. The plan was received with appreciation and the senior executives requested additional details about sales in all pilot banking centers.

At this same time frame, the beginning of a major economic downturn was hitting the country, starting in some of these same key markets that were targeted for implementation of the new role. For a while, a so called "flight to quality" (2009 and again in 2020)[18] brought rapid growth into the bank, including dramatic increases in small business banking. However, the senior executives saw this sector as a growing risk for increased investment, so the division president decided to pull the pilot back and discontinue the implementation.

As Tenicia explained this to the project team, the news was met with great disappointment, but with understanding due to recognition of the growing financial crisis. She reassured the team, "The new role and process have been proven as effective, but the timing is just not right."

No one could have foreseen the length of the recession, but it took nearly a decade. As the economic recovery began, small businesses once again became an important and growing set of customers who needed financial services. Some of the original project team members were contacted by new division leaders to review what had been developed but not fully implemented years earlier.

The economy had changed, and technology had advanced so some of the design was outdated. However, the supporting functions based on financial needs were still valuable and effective. Some revisions and updates were made and then the role, the products and services, and the playbook were all launched nationally.

The development and implementation cycle during the economic recovery went much faster based on the previous work and this became a competitive advantage. At the time about one in four consumer households had some type of small business so the ability to service their combined financial needs was a success. The goal of 15 percent revenue growth was realized and their U.S. small business banking market share grew to about 9 percent. Owner relationship surveys indicated satisfaction with both products and services. Facilitating processes prove to be a worthy investment in a rapidly changing environment.

Chapter Six Summary

- A small business banking example

- At first, we failed in achieving the objective because we focused mainly on the value stream steps alone, and many of the solutions were in the enabling processes
- When implementation was paused due to an economic recession, the restart several years later still benefited from the design

Chapter Seven

"Are you playing football or fútbol?"

Residential Flooring Installer

Earlier, I described experiences that were mainly reactive to a failure mode or a known problem. Here, we move from defense to offense at a residential flooring installer. Mahesh and Faiza own M and F Renovations that specializes in new and replacement flooring. When they decided to start the company, they both agreed to provide a high-quality customer experience with the end-to-end process and the end product. Their initial design of the business focused on effective value stream steps with the customer at the center, and a set of facilitating practices to ensure quality and clear communication.

It just happens that both Mahesh and Faiza passionately enjoy fútbol—or what some countries refer to as soccer. In fútbol, the players have to constantly transition between defense and attack. Contrast this with American football where each team has a separate defensive and offensive unit, so they do not fluidly move between offense and defense as teams do in the game of fútbol. Are you playing football or fútbol? I ask this question because it is worth determining whether or not you are flexible to assess the current risks and failure modes, and also to anticipate potential risks and failure modes. If you are approaching your craft as an American football team defensive unit, you could focus only on reacting to failures and errors as they occur. But if you approach your enterprise as a fútbol team, you simultaneously look for both the current failure modes (reacting as a defensive unit) and anticipated failure modes (as an attack unit). M and F Renovations focused on both the known and the anticipated failure modes simultaneously. They implemented process controls into the end-to-end value stream by adding critical supporting components.

Their value stream process steps include:

- Generate customer leads
- Engage with the potential customer
- Consult with the prospective customer to discuss their desires
- Visit the customer location and measure the flooring area
- Offer samples of different flooring options to the customer
- Provide cost and schedule estimates for the options
- Assist the customer in making a final decision
- Send the customer a contract proposal
- Receive the signed contract and deposit from the customer
- Schedule the work
- Deliver materials to the worksite
- Complete the work
- Receive the final balance due from the customer

The facilitating processes include:

- Conduct marketing and advertising
- Establish material distributor relationships

- Develop consulting relationships with interior designers
- Contract with flooring installation laborers
- Create cost and estimation calculators
- Organize accounting and financial management functions
- Maintain liability insurance
- Implement quality standards and inspections
- Perform control checkpoints

I wish to emphasize the last two on the list of enabling activities. Mahesh and Faiza determined where to insert the control checks in their value stream process to ensure high quality and to reduce waste. The three main control points are: (1) follow up with the customer after they receive the estimate to answer any additional questions or concerns, (2) have the customer check the materials delivered to the work address to verify that they are the correct materials, and (3) inspect the completed work in a walkthrough with the customer.

For jobs taking longer than three days, the owners visit the job site midway through the work to ensure that it is proceeding correctly and to address any questions. A set of standards are used to include the fit of the flooring, a check on the floor level, matching heights to adjoining floor surfaces, and that the correct floor finish is achieved.

In the final customer walkthrough, Mahesh and Faiza validate with the customer that the work met or exceeded expectations, provide cleaning and maintenance guidance to the homeowner, ask for references, and encourage the customers to write an online review of their experience. It is another demonstration of being on both defense (validating that the work is satisfactory) and offense (asking for references) in this quality control facilitating process.

The Value of Being on Offense

To explain the value of these control points, let me share one situation that happened with M and F Renovations. Skylar was a customer who selected a vinyl luxury tile for her kitchen floor. When the materials arrived at Skylar's home, she was asked by Faiza to verify that the delivered flooring tile was correct. She discovered that although it was the correct type of tile, it was not the correct color and pattern she had picked. This simple control check prevented the installers from putting in the wrong flooring which would have cost M and F Renovations the subsequent removal and then a second install with the correct flooring. If this mistake had occurred, their contract may have gone from a profitable to an unprofitable job and could have damaged their reputation. The delay in the schedule due to replacing the incorrect flooring could have had a domino effect on their upcoming jobs.

There is a cost to completing these control points and this does add to the cost of M and F Renovations' work. However, these controls ensure the customer experience and the high-quality end product that Mahesh and Faiza agreed to provide. If managed well, the cost of the controls is offset by avoiding mistakes and waste.

Although you will react to numerous failure modes in your business similar to ones I have described, I also encourage you to anticipate what could go wrong and proactively implement facilitating functions that prevent errors and failures in your value stream process.

Brief Description of Risk and Opportunity Assessment

In chapter three, I introduced the risk and opportunity assessment. I will briefly revisit it here and add some insights based on M and F Renovations' use of this method.

- You can see above that Mahesh and Faiza wrote out their value stream process with the customer in mind.

- They then thought through the possible failure modes and errors that could happen, and they paid attention to decisions and handoffs. As in fútbol, they were playing both offense and defense by considering what they already knew and by asking "what if" questions to identify opportunities and innovation.

- They rated each failure mode and opportunity for significance, likelihood of occurrence, and how quickly that would be able to react.

- This led to a ranking from greatest to lowest significance.

- One of their decisions was to avoid costly mistakes by adding control points to ensure accuracy and high quality.

If you were looking for someone local to install flooring and you found ratings and reviews for M and F Renovations, you would read literally hundreds of reviews describing the way they interact with customers and check for quality. It has earned them five-star ratings and increased their revenue. Compared with some of their competitors, it is obvious that they pay attention to details and avoid mistakes. These relatively simple steps make them stand out in their field. They made modest investments in the right places to strengthen their business process backbone.

The next few chapters examine large-scale facilitating systems that have within themselves, value stream and enabling components. I detail the work we did to avoid an eleventh failure in a row with semiconductor manufacturing training. This was where I first discovered the vital importance of foundational processes. You will then learn about how we designed a change management lifecycle. You may be able to draw in some of what we developed in both of these efforts to directly apply in your organization.

Chapter Seven Summary

- A local residential flooring small business example
- Take a proactive approach to evaluating your risks and opportunities
- Create competitive advantage

Chapter Eight

"No number eleven!"

Training—Part 1

In a senior executive meeting at a global semiconductor company, an air of frustration was in the room when the topic turned to manufacturing associate training . . . again. It always shows up as a deficiency in manufacturing productivity studies, in safety audits, and in employee satisfaction surveys. The managers intuitively knew, and nearly all executives do, that there is enormous opportunity through improved training. But, how to do it right?

And, how to sustain it?

They described several attempts at improved training across the line of business and their eight locations but readily admitted that no one had really gotten it right. Programs would be started and make quick progress but then just as quickly fade away—only to have their reputation abased at the next audit when once again, training was highlighted as an issue. Finally, one of the executives raised his voice and said, "We've tried addressing the problems of associate training ten times before and we failed every time! What's going to make this time different?"[19]

A team was formed with representatives from each of the manufacturing locations and after hearing about the executive meeting and the complaint of having failed ten times before, we adopted the mantra "No Number Eleven!" The team was fully dedicated to solving the training problem with a process that addressed the systemic issues and that was sustainable. In a fast-paced, complex, cost-sensitive worldwide manufacturing setting, this was not a small challenge.

The onboarding and training experience tells you a lot about your new employer. It can make an enormous difference in productivity, safety, regulatory compliance, and reducing associate turn over. Virtually any organization provides training in one way or another. For many, it is left to the experienced associates and managers to do the best they can to train new associates or to cross-train existing associates. It goes on each day at some level. But why is it so hard to provide effective training? Why do so few businesses do it well? Is it worth the investment?

A leader was charged with forming a worldwide manufacturing excellence team to address the need for sustainable improvement. I was asked to lead the team. We did not realize it when the team first formed, but this journey of discovery and development would take our team of ten members more than two years. Neither did we realize just how remarkably effective we would be and that the process we developed could have application in a wide variety of training settings, and with the benefit of our learning, can be done in significantly less time. If you need to improve training, perhaps you can save time and benefit from our design. The key was the determination that there would be "No number eleven" failure!

Organizing the Team

The leadership team assigned the effort to the Manufacturing Excellence (MX) executive who then selected a program manager to assemble and lead a team with representatives from each of the worldwide manufacturing locations. This team came to be known as the Worldwide Manufacturing Excellence Team (MX Team) with a mandate to standardize operational practices and processes across the entire division. Several factors combined to make this team effective. First, the location representatives were selected from associates in roles that were close to the manufacturing line, so they had first-hand knowledge of the current training environment and the related challenges. These team members were passionate about improving training. Second, the MX executive set a tone of being candid and honest, so each team member was comfortable describing challenges and expressing opinions. Third, emphasis was placed on developing a repeatable process that would be sustained and improved rather than another one-time event. The story of the executive meeting was told to the location representatives, and they adopted the mantra, "No number eleven!" Fourth, the worldwide MX training team met together in person several times each year over a period of two years. These meetings were hosted by the various manufacturing locations so that the team was able to tour the location and meet with manufacturing associates as part of the week-long team meeting. This kept a sense of reality and reminded the team members that they had to be the advocates for the manufacturing associates. In between the team meetings, conference calls were held to build out detailed plans and complete project work.

Define the Objective

In addition to no number eleven failure, we defined the objectives to achieve clean audit results and stakeholder satisfaction. The stakeholders included the direct production team members, front-line production managers, senior leaders, product engineers, and quality engineers. For baseline information we only had qualitative and anecdotal feedback through audit defects and employee surveys. This alone should have been a flag that the process was not being managed because there were no metrics in place.

As-Is Process Study and Findings

The first major phase of the project was to conduct a worldwide needs assessment and study of our current training at each location. The MX training program manager traveled to the sites and worked with the local representative to conduct focus group sessions. Small groups of manufacturing operators were invited to participate in these forums where they responded to basic questions about the effectiveness of the current training and methods. The program manager held one-on-one interviews with site managers and executives to get their assessment of training at their location and to determine what was most important to them. One of our favorite management interview questions was "Who owns the training process at your site?" Based on the array of answers, we could only conclude that no one owned training. All comments were captured and compiled into a database. Upon completion of these initial focus group sessions and management interviews, just over 1,500 comments had been documented across the entire division. The worldwide MX training team met to review and distill the comments into common themes and the frequency that each theme occurred. We added feedback and findings from the audits and a Pareto analysis revealed the top detractors to be (1) the lack of resource planning that led to conflicts between training and production activities, (2) inadequate training materials, and (3) poorly selected and unqualified trainers (figure 3).

One of the more interesting discoveries from this work is that regardless of country or culture, the detractors were the same. The manufacturing locations were in the United States, Canada, France, Italy, Ireland, Japan, and Singapore. We had sites that claimed to have addressed these issues, but upon further investigation, we found that they were handled as events and not systemic improvements. Again, and again, we found evidence of short-lived solutions and no

Figure 3. Pareto

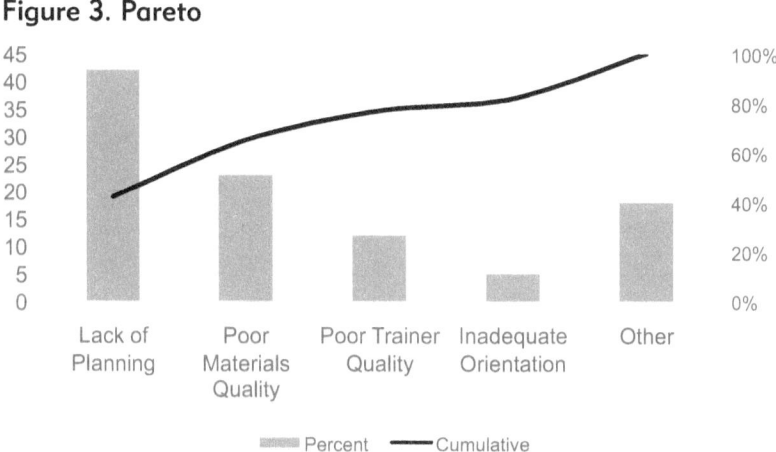

evidence of sustained performance. In most cases, a changing of the guard took place and managers who promoted training moved to new positions and were replaced with managers who were competent in their main responsibilities, but who were not so inclined to place as much emphasis on training. The quality of training would decline. In the Capability Maturity Model developed by the Carnegie Mellon University Software Engineering Institute, this phenomenon is described as the lowest level of maturity. It can further be labeled as "ad hoc" or a hero environment where success depends on a champion leader. When that hero is replaced with another leader, the level of support most often suffers. This decline can happen in a surprisingly short time. We saw this happen within weeks of the management change.

As we mapped out the process at each location and looked at them side by side, they all had the basic value stream steps of (1) corporate/site orientation, (2) department/sector orientation, (3) on-the-job training (OJT), (4) certification, and (5) certification tracking and management. Rarely did we see any mention of resource planning. Occasionally, we saw practices that addressed training materials and a train-the-trainer program, but these appeared to be events that were not part of ongoing, sustained efforts. Materials were created but then not maintained.

We discovered that while doing a relatively good job with the value steam, we were almost entirely neglecting the enabling processes. As we described our findings to the leadership team, this brought clarity to the root cause problems and led to focusing on creating and implementing the missing supporting functions. We followed the same structure of actions outlined in chapter three.

Evaluating the current state revealed, to no one's surprise, an internal organization at the "initial" stage of process development per the Capability Maturity Model Integration—a state it had been in for thirty years. The team determined that it would have to develop its own prototype nearly from scratch. It would take a pilot project to prove the feasibility of a "Repeatable" OJT model and set the stage for creating a "defined" level process.[20]

Many enterprises have implemented total quality, Baldridge performance excellence, and other similar methods through which they gained value, but then declined and lost much of their value. I have often wondered why some great businesses that made large investments would go through dramatic downturns within a few years after implementing these methods. They include Motorola, General Electric, Allied Signal/Honeywell, Circuit City, Home Depot, Daimler/Chrysler, and many others. There is evidence that the methodologies and data-driven approach used in quality management and design are effective, but why then was company after company going through serious and destructive losses? I now believe that one of the mistakes contributing to this type of loss is the confusion between value stream and facilitating activities, and the resulting incorrect application of the quality management methodologies. If you focus mainly or exclusively on the value stream and neglect the backbone, you will not sustain the improvements nor endure through the turbulence. Worse yet, you may incorrectly create the value stream to be too stable and inflexible. You could become unresponsive to changing customer expectations and competitive conditions.

In the case study of the worldwide manufacturing training effort, the team discovered that while the value stream had received a lot of attention and was the focus of previous attempts to improve training, it was the lack of well-defined enabling processes that was the root cause of the problem and offered the opportunity for a breakthrough improvement.

Chapter Eight Summary

- We first discovered the importance of facilitating processes and backbone structures in this large-scale manufacturing training initiative
- Our team united around the mantra "no number eleven" failure
- Define your objective in terms of a success metric
- Document what you know about the gap between your baseline performance and your objective
- Conduct in-depth root cause analysis and include facilitating processes

Chapter Nine

"Facilitating process steps were missing."

Training—Part 2

Value Stream Process

For context, I will briefly describe the training value stream. If you need to improve your training, you may get direct use from what we defined, otherwise, just look for the kind of design you need to develop in your facilitating processes.

Value stream step 1.
On Board to Corporation / Site

1.1 Welcome associate

1.2 Process HR documents

1.3 Issue identification badge, card

1.4 Explain pay, policies, benefits

1.5 Provide overview of the corporation and site that includes products, services, customers, and organizational structure

Value stream step 2.
On Board to Department / Sector

2.1 Introduce to team members and key contacts

2.2 Walk through the high-level flow with emphasis on inputs and outputs

2.3 Cover the training roadmap with emphasis on details for first week

Value stream step 3.
Train on the Job

3.1 Explain the competency profile as a framework for the training roadmap

3.2 Describe the certification criteria, requirements, and expected timeline

3.3 Complete the training roadmap activities

Value stream step 4.
Certify Operator

4.1 Conduct written test

4.2 Conduct hands-on test

4.3 Certify trainee

Value stream step 5.
Track Certification

5.1 Enter certification event information

5.2 Track and report all certified team members by operation/role

Robust Facilitating Processes

The worldwide MX training team met in a week-long workshop to develop the framework of a solution. We reviewed all the findings to date, took note of the best practices we had identified, and then started a "white board" session to build out the new workflow, including the facilitating process steps that were missing from our training.

Based on the current state assessment, we identified the need for three new sub-processes; (6) "Plan Training Resources," (7) "Develop Training Materials," and (8) "Select and Develop Trainers." To these we added a fourth which we titled (9) "Manage the Process." This fourth enabling function addressed the need to establish overall ownership and metrics, determine the organizational structure, clearly define the roles and responsibilities, and create a continuous improvement cycle of change management. These four foundational processes support the entire end-to-end value stream (figure 4).

Figure 4. Training Process Value Stream and Facilitating Processes

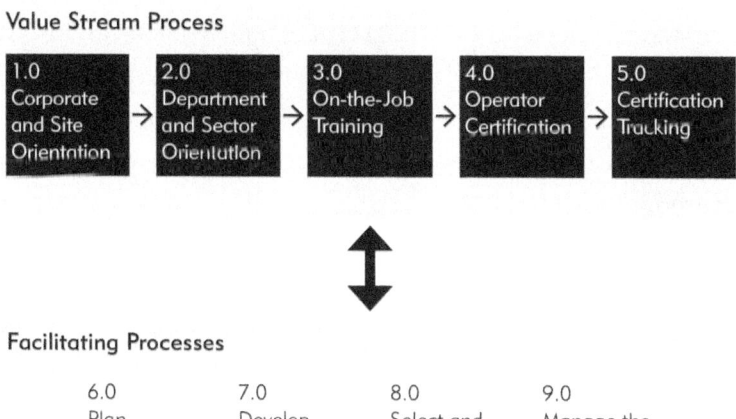

Next, I will give details of the four enabling activities that we created. These sub-processes are the critical fix to our plaguing failure modes. As you read through these, consider how to evaluate your own facilitating operations.

Sub-process 6.
Plan Training Resources

Objective: Allocate resources to staff the organization with trainers, certifiers, and an adult learning specialist.

Process Steps

6.1 Define roles and responsibilities for trainers, certifiers, training coordinators, and adult learning specialists.

6.2 Estimate the required training resources based on incoming associates and planned cross-training as associates move from job to job or take on additional roles.

6.1 Define Roles

Roles were defined and organized. In smaller organizations one person may fill multiple roles. In larger organizations several people may be required for each of the roles. In the case of our manufacturing line, we assigned some of these as full-time roles within each of our production teams.

A line with approximately 500 associates would generally have one of the executives who acted as the process owner in addition to normal production executive responsibilities. One of the second line managers who reported into the process owner fulfilled the process manager role, again in addition to normal production management responsibilities.

The training coordinators were full-time roles and often cover a span of about 200 associates. For a production line with

500 associates, two or three coordinators are required. During the initial implementation, more coordinators could be utilized because they tend to become the constraint during development of new training materials (refer to Sub-process 7, Develop Training Material).

A master trainer is assigned to take ownership of the training documentation for each specific job. This role of master trainer would best fit with one of the more experienced associates who can act as a mentor to others and who can make decisions based on strong experience and thorough knowledge of the job content. In small organizations with only one or two people in each role, one associate may be selected as master trainer for several jobs.

Trainers are selected based on two main criteria. First, they must be experienced associates who model the kind of skills and attitudes desired in other associates. Second, they should be interested in training. We found that while many highly skilled associates were models of what we desired to instill in other associates, not all of them wanted to train others. We learned that it was best to not expect these associates to provide training because they became impatient and ineffective in teaching others. They were often better utilized to concentrate their additional efforts on production improvements, quality assurance, safety, or other such functions in addition to their regular production roles. The trainers that we selected because they enjoyed training had the right attitude and worked best with trainees. They also contributed to the ongoing improvement of training because they were more personally invested and enjoyed seeing their ideas implemented.

6.2 Estimate the required training resources

The team agreed upon an algorithm to calculate the annual training time requirement based on each location's hiring profile, growth, and turn over. This algorithm included cross-training requirements for associates who move to a different job or who take on additional responsibilities. In generic terms, the calculation requires inputs of the current population, anticipated annual changes in the population, turn over due to redeployment and attrition, and the anticipated cross-training. With these inputs, each production area calculated the total number of new certifications expected during the upcoming year. By multiplying the number of planned certifications by a weighted average number of hours for training on each production operation, a department calculates the total number of hours and the number of trainers required for training. The output of this algorithm is an input to the staffing plan for the location and directly supports resource planning for line managers.

Generically, you could think of this algorithm as the following equation:

$$(((P \times (G + T + A)) \times H) / TH) / W = FTE$$

Where:

P = total current associate population

G = anticipated change in population as percent growth (+) or percent reduction (−) in population during the plan year

T = percent of turn-over in the population due to redeployment and cross training during the plan year

A = percent of attrition anticipated during the plan year

H = average number of total hours required for training per job (see Sub-process 7)

TH = average number of hours per week that each trainer would be expected to devote to training as a part of their regular job

W = hours per week for a full-time-equivalent (FTE) associate

FTE = number of full-time-equivalent trainers required for the plan year

As a scenario, if I had a population of 120 associates with expected growth of 3 percent, expected redeployment and cross training of 18 percent, 2 percent expected attrition, an average training duration of 65 hours per job, trainers who are expected to spend 10 hours of their week providing training, and a work week based on 40 hours, I would calculate my required training resources for the plan year as follows:

$(120 *(0.03 +0.18 +0.02)) * 65) / 10) / 40 = 4.49$ FTE trainers.

The site training process manager tracks the average time required for training on each operation. The project uses this baseline in the annual training time algorithm as well as to set the individual baseline against which to track new hire training time reduction. Although training time has been reduced overall by more than 50 percent, for some individual production steps the new training effort now requires more time. Although, the project continues to place the highest value on stakeholder satisfaction, the potential for reduced training time and improved quality solidified the program's acceptance throughout the division.

Nearly any serious effort to improve training is likely to significantly reduce training time, and the 50 percent reduction is not at all unique to this specific approach to training. What is extraordinary is to then sustain the training time reduction and simultaneous benefits in quality and effectiveness.

Sub-process 7.
Develop Training Material

Objective: Develop training materials that are effective, practical, easily maintained, easily shared across locations, and which have a consistent format.

Process Steps

7.1 Select a job to document.

7.2 Choose six to eight participants with varying levels of skills for the job.

7.3 Assign ownership to maintain the training and certification materials.

7.4 Schedule a "competency profile" workshop.

7.5 Conduct the workshop to document the job skills and training plan outline.

7.6 Resolve any outstanding issues exposed during the workshop.

7.7 Finalize the training materials.

7.8 Approve the training materials.

7.9 Determine the certification standard.

7.10 Approve the certification standard.

A database should be selected for the training documentation and can be as simple as excel spreadsheets or as elaborate as an enterprise server database. It should be universally available to associates and allow links to other existing documentation for training and daily tasks.

Training materials consist mainly of a competency profile and a training plan outline for each operation, position, or tool. A team of knowledgeable associates creates the materials as a group by attending a workshop facilitated by an adult learning specialist or training coordinator. These teams bring a mix of skill levels from the most experienced to those recently trained, although optional attendees include supporting specialists such as engineers or technicians. Representatives from different shifts or departments/locations who perform the same job should be included. A "master trainer" is selected

Figure 5. Competency Profile

	1	2	3	4
A. Introduction	Manager	Department Mission	Team Members	Assigned Operation
B. Safety	Emergency Exits	First Response	Chemical Safety	Safety Equipment
C. Systems	email account	Control System	Logistical System	Technology Help Desk
D. Operation	Product Handling	Loading Product	Processing Product	Unloading Product
Quality	Standards	Process Controls		

Figure 6. Module D2 Loading Product

Elements/Training Steps	Trainer's Explanation	Learner's Demonstration
1. Setup and Load	Demonstrate how to: • Select product • Explain the setup Show how to: • Set up contactor • Complete temperature check • Orient product tray • Use SmarTest	• Perform the setup • Verify product handler is correct • Explain the verification data • Load the product • Correctly use SmarTest
Conducted: Hands On Time Needed: v2.0 Hours		

Figure 7. Training Plan Outline

Day 3	Activity	Hands on Activity?	Mode	Duration
	Review of Day 2	No	Formal	1 Hour
D3	Processing Product	Yes	OJT	2 Hours
D4	Unloading Product	Yes	Shadow	1.5 Hours
E2	Process Controls	No	Formal	1.5 Hours
D3	Processing Product	Yes	Practice	2 Hours

to take ownership of the training materials and be responsible for ongoing updates. The time required to complete a profile is dependent on the team's experience with the process and the availability of materials to repurpose. Initial workshops can take as long as four days, but experienced groups may take less than a day. Often, there is content that is created by the earlier groups that can be applied to the remaining jobs as they are documented. Shared training competencies could include the video conferencing application used by an entire company as well as production systems used by large parts of the organization.

As the training for each position is profiled, this group of six to eight participants first creates a matrix of general competencies (designated with letters) and specific competencies, or skills, (designated with numbers) like the example in figure 5. The matrix can be expanded to fit the various skills and topics required for a job. If a general competency has more than 6 specific competencies, break the topic into more than one general competency.

Look at row D, Operation. Reading across, you will see product handling, loading product, processing product, and unloading product as the specific competencies within the general competency of operation. For each cell in the competency profile matrix, a second document for a specific competency lists the training element, and within the training element, trainer and trainee performance objectives.

Drilling down on D2, Loading Product from the competency profile, let us look at one training step within that competency. In figure 6, we see that D2 Loading Product includes Setup and Load. For each element, we describe what the trainer explains and then what the learner should demonstrate. Production versions of the on-line documentation for a specific competency often include links to online production resources and procedure documents.

Following the analysis of competencies, the team writes a training plan outline to sequence the schedule for training a new hire on that specific operation (figure 7). This one shows the training expectations for day 3 of the training. The columns show the sequencing of the competency profile cells, whether or not the activity is conducted hands-on, the training strategy or mode, and an approximate time allocation for the specific competency. During training, competencies and tasks are taught several times with increasing proficiency and involvement expected of the trainee as training progresses through the training modes.

The team creating the training plan outline can be specific down to the element level or leave choices up to the trainer to determine based on conditions at the time of the training. Whenever relevant, imbed tips and reminders that assist trainers in both the training plan outline and specific competency details.

To simplify the concept of training strategies, the project defined five training modes for use with the training plan outline. Trainers are expected to incorporate the modes and training techniques to match the trainee's learning style, and to use all modes for each specific competency.

The modes are:

SOJT: Structured on-the-job training includes demonstrations, guided performance, or scripted activities occurring on the job.

We defined this sequence for SOJT:

Step 1. Trainer describes the task to the trainee.

Step 2. Trainer demonstrates the task to the trainee.

Step 3. Trainee describes the task back to the trainer.

Step 4. Trainer instructs the trainee to do the task.

Step 5. Trainee does the task while closely supervised by the trainer.

Practice: Job tasks that have been trained using SOJT are now completed by the trainee under trainer supervision.

Validate: The trainer checks the trainee's work against the certification standards, gives feedback and plans remedial training for the trainee if standards are not met. Once a trainee is performing a task to standard, the topic no longer needs to be addressed in training except when competencies are revalidated.

Generally, the documented portion of a training plan outline covers the first several days of training. This takes the trainee up to a point where a first round "validation" event can be recommended. After that point, the trainer can customize the training to meet the needs of the trainee and still balance training with production requirements. The remainder of the on-the-job training emphasizes practical experience until the trainee has finished all the competencies to standards and is ready for certification. After the point of certification, continued training enables the new associate to become more proficient and to resolve uncommon problems.

All training materials are created, maintained, and accessed through a suite of databases shared across the team. All users need access to the materials from all locations. Training coordinators may re-use materials created elsewhere, and materials may be seamlessly migrated between sites doing similar tasks.

These training materials were deemed to be of "sufficient" depth for the structured on-the-job training (SOJT) documentation. The development methodology derives from classic Instructional System Design ("ISD") principles for task and skills analysis, although the focus is not on "task" performance per-se, but rather a mixture of knowledge and skills required for certification. Scope for each competency is easily understood because each can be packaged readily to meet the on-the-spot training needs of the team. Procedures are expressly prohibited from being part of any profile documentation—they are linked or referenced instead so that there is one source of the current version. Operational areas were encouraged to develop additional training materials for trainers only on an "as-needed basis" for critical skill areas or for stable common skills like technology systems.

Competency profiling workshops routinely reveal problems with procedures or inconsistencies between team member practices. A workshop participant, designated as the master trainer, assumes responsibility to resolve these issues after the workshop while a training coordinator tracks resolution. Certification requirements are derived from the profile by the master trainer and in consultation with the training coordinator. In smaller business applications, one person may fill multiple roles and determine the training content and the certification requirements.

Sub-process 8.
Select and Develop Trainers

Objective: Select trainers based on job skills and attitudes and then develop their training skills to effectively conduct training.

Process Steps

8.1 Determine the number of required trainers.

8.2 Screen candidates based on job skills and attitudes.

8.3 Develop training skills through a "train-the-trainer" course.

8.4 Certify trainers through observation during practical exercises of training.

The team divided trainer skills into three attributes: technical job skills, interest and attitude, and training skills. Selection is based on the first two, job skills and interest and attitude. Managers use an interview guide to select trainers.

Trainers acquire or augment the third attribute, training skills, through a "train-the-trainer" class and ongoing interactions with master trainers, training coordinators, and adult learning specialists. New trainers must meet a set of supervision requirements. The requirements for the MX "Train-the-Trainer" (TTT) class came out of a workshop held during the pilot phase. This workshop followed the competency profile workshop and training plan outline development process. Adult learning specialists, master trainers, and training coordinators representing all sites took part in the requirements workshop. A sub-team developed the initial "Conducting on-the-job Training" class based on the training plan outline.

During the class, expert instructors repeatedly model the same training techniques that the participants are expected to use to train associates. This modeling activity is a real challenge for the instructor in a group setting and should be conducted by highly skilled, experienced trainers selected and prepared by the Adult Learning Specialist.

The course includes the following topics:

- Plan, prepare and manage training
- Communicate the purpose of MX processes
- Use the MX training databases
- Use training materials
- Schedule training activities
- Facilitate learning
- Create a positive learning environment
- Improve communication skills
- Apply adult learning principles and techniques
- Use instructional techniques

- Evaluate learning & skills
- Describe the importance of certification
- Assess trainee skills
- Continuously assess learning
- Validate that the trainee is ready for certification
- Conduct a training session with peer input

This Train-the-Trainer course and a corporate diversity, equity, and inclusion training class are the only formal training programs required for each trainer. However, for scheduling convenience and tracking, the competency profile workshops may be scheduled as "classes" using an existing class scheduling program.

The development plan, SOJT methods, and on-line methodology set the stage for achieving the "Defined" maturity level as characterized in the Capability Maturity Model.

Sub-process 9.
Manage the Process

Objective: Establish ownership, success metrics, and accountability for the training process.

Process Steps

9.1 Establish the training process owner.

9.2 Determine the key metrics.

9.3 Establish the baseline for the key metrics.

9.4 Track progress to the metrics.

9.5 Manage the continuous improvement of the process.

The global MX team created and maintained policies and procedures to provide descriptions of the facilitating activities, roles, responsibilities, implementation guidelines, and change management for continuous improvement. They also specified metrics for quantifying ownership, system deployment, stakeholder satisfaction feedback, and new hire training time. The policies and procedures are created at the line of business level and then specific addendums can be created at the site or team level.

The location executive manager now assigns ownership of training to specific managers. These management owners select process managers and training coordinators to schedule implementation and coordinate logistics. The department manager assigns ownership of training materials to a master trainer for each operation. In most cases, managers and production operators fill these roles as part-time assignments in addition to other job tasks. Compliance with the metrics is now firmly established.

The average duration of training is defined as the time between the start of training and the point of certification. In figure 8, you will see that the average training duration was reduced by more than 50 percent and then sustained by implementing these facilitating processes.

Figure 8. Average Training Duration

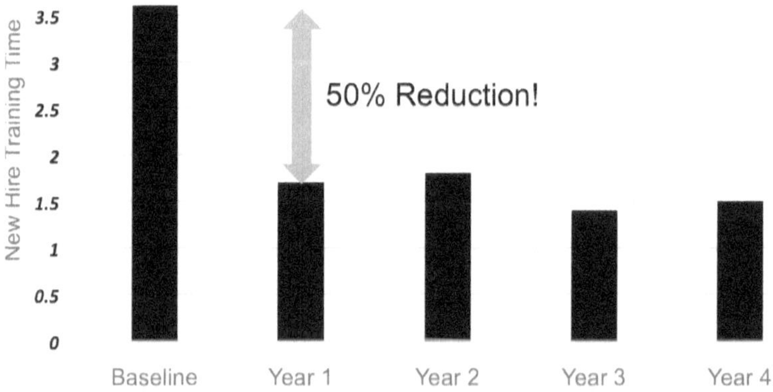

This reduction in training time was not the original objective but is a significant benefit in cost savings of human resource and an improvement to productivity.

Training coordinators compile and report the metrics quarterly for each location and then roll up the data for the division. Management owners hold reviews with middle managers at each location and with executive management.

Chapter Nine Summary

- The solution to the manufacturing training failures included defining the value stream and facilitating operations
- You may be able to directly use some of our training process to develop yours

Chapter Ten

*"After more than a decade,
it was still in place and being constantly improved."*

Training—Part 3

Conducting a Pilot

We tested at one production line in one location to determine the effectiveness and to identify deficiencies. This pilot team was overzealous in their first attempt at documenting the required training. They created detailed guides and content that quickly became outdated and too burdensome to maintain. Further, it was not practical for use by the trainers and the trainees. We learned to keep the training documentation light and depend on the production procedures to hold the details. We gained experience in conducting competency profile workshops as described in Sub-process 7, "Develop Training Material." After several sessions of these, we hit a stride where they became more fluid and effective. Each competency profile represents one job or role. We learned to have one of the subject matter experts from a previous competency profile session attend the first session for a new competency profile. Their experience led the new workshop team to learn quickly. Several of the competencies were shared across all operational positions such as the manufacturing logistics control system, email, and safety. Once developed, these could simply be reused in the other competency profiles.

We knew that we had to develop a training materials and content database and that all production team members and trainers needed access. But we also anticipated that we would have to grow into this database once we finished the test because of the time required to develop it and the anticipated evolution towards a final plan. The pilot started with a manual method for storing the training information and we found this to be ineffective. Therefore, while still in the pilot, we accelerated the development and deployment of the training materials database.

We tested for three months and were able to see the first candidates earn their certifications. There was increasing pressure from the leadership team to quickly implement, but we encouraged them to accept the testing timeline and then allow for improvement. After the updates were developed, we then implemented at each of the worldwide locations with a staggered schedule where a location had three weeks to kick off their implementation before we started the next location.

A completely defined change management workflow was included with the rollout for governance and to allow for continual updates based on our experience. This change management process is like the one built for the Customer Profitability team described in chapter eleven.

Results

Metrics

The metrics used to monitor success include the average new hire training time (figure 8) and stakeholder satisfaction (figure 9). We also tracked safety and quality audits for issues. These metrics indicate the ongoing effectiveness and, in part, the financial return in terms of labor savings and workforce flexibility. Referring to figure 8 for stakeholders, the quality of training jumped from Very Dissatisfied in the baseline period prior to implementing the new training process, to well into the Very Satisfied range after implementation. This higher satisfaction level was sustained with a gradual increase throughout the next 7 survey periods and beyond.

Stakeholder Satisfaction

The original objective for this body of work was to improve training for entry-level production associates and to sustain it through continuous improvement. In a phrase, it was to have "no number eleven failure!" After several years we saw sustained success and the process continued to evolve through continuous improvement. This was the first time in the history of the division that entry-level production team member training was no longer highlighted as an associate satisfaction issue, nor on the hot list of safety and audit issues. If training got mentioned at all, there were now operational owners to address these issues. Furthermore, the success led other

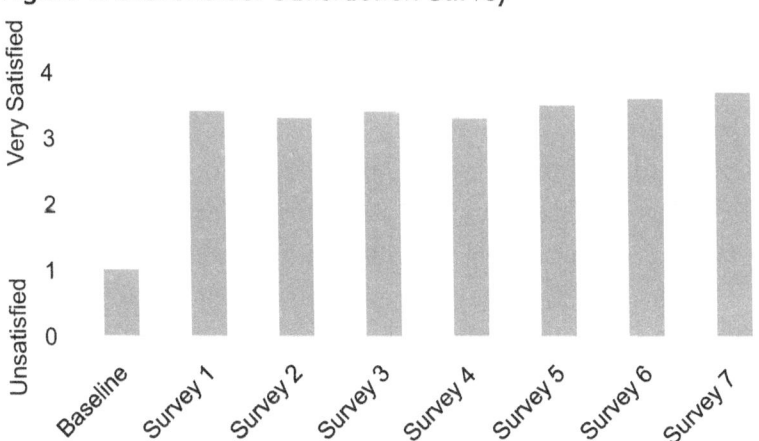

Figure 9. Stakeholder Satisfaction Survey

groups to approach the MX Training Team to implement a similar design for engineering and shared services teams.

Planning

Training time had been assumed within the current staffing models with a simple percent of FTE along with other factors such as vacation and other absences. The facilitating process for planning, (Sub-process 6. Plan Training Resources), provided a more accurate and truthful approach to account for the time required by both trainers and trainees to accomplish training and certification. This improved the staffing levels and addressed the constant complaint that trainers were expected to simultaneously perform their full production duties and provide new hire and cross training. The reduction in training time offset some of this additional FTE impact. It became visible to management who could now plan with confidence.

Training Time

With the greater than 50 percent reduction in time from start date to certification on their first assigned operation, the benefits were twofold. First, the new hire achieved the expected level of productivity much quicker. Second, by using the training competency profile, training materials, and training roadmap, there was less drag on the trainer's time. Trainers are typically strong producers and for every hour they are used as trainers, they are less productive on their own assigned work. By reducing the training cycle time for new hires, these trainers could return to full productivity sooner. Because training had not been accurately accounted for in the staffing levels, there was a trade off in the time required to provide training. The enterprise had been absorbing the cost of training in lower productivity, but now the training time was known and factored into the staffing model. This led to a small net decrease in the required number of

FTE (full-time equivalent) associates. Managers were understandably reluctant to accept the lower FTE targets for each department, but executives approved the new staffing levels. These reductions were realized through attrition and by not back-filling some of the positions as associates moved to new roles.

The management team at our manufacturing site in Bromont, Quebec, Canada, conducted a study of the time it takes for a new hire to train and become proficient. They found a pattern that provided two key insights to the training cycle time. First, they noted that a candidate is certified on a specific operation at about a seventy-percent proficiency level. Second, they found that the time it takes to reach the point of certification is nearly equal to the time between certification and achieving mastery. In other words, certification occurs at the mid-point of the entire training cycle (figure 10). The time between certification and achieving mastery depends on the associate experiencing the less frequent and more unusual events which require greater knowledge, and which often require the associate to call on additional resources for assistance. The main reduction in cycle time was realized between the start of training and the point of certification.

Figure 10. Trainee Proficiency

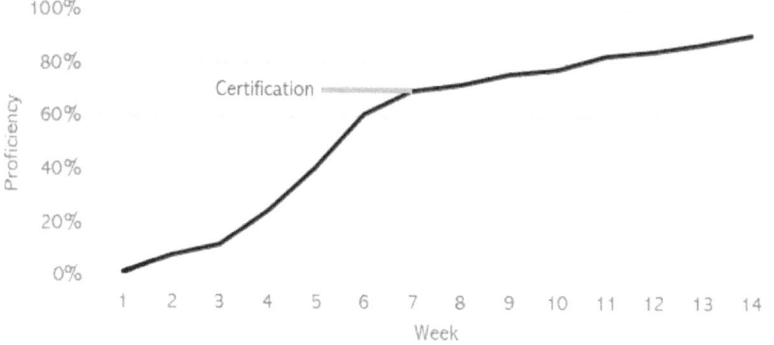

Another benefit to training time reduction is the flexibility of the workforce. The process improved the cross training of associates to learn additional operations and enabled managers to move associates from job to job as needed to meet production schedules and cover absences. Although the reduction in training time was not as significant for cross training, it was more efficient than previous practices. Associates became familiar with the standard formatting of training materials which made it easier to move from one production position to another. They could access the training materials database and reference training materials for any operation to which they were assigned.

Quality

The measurement of quality was selected as a secondary metric. Secondary metrics are generally in opposition to the primary metric, thus protecting the enterprise from a gain in speed at the expense of lower quality—or some similar trade off. In the manufacturing environment, it is difficult to directly attribute product quality to training because there are numerous other variables. On-going manufacturing improvements and equipment changes can affect quality more than training. However, by monitoring product quality, we saw no decline while implementing training, and therefore were satisfied that we had not compromised quality at the expense of reducing the training cycle time. It could even be possible to improve quality because of improved training, but this was never proven in our setting due to the difficulty of singling out training as a variable with so many other changes that also impact quality.

Cost

A cost-benefit analysis showed that it takes about a one-year initial investment to organize and implement the training process. By year two, the benefits outweighed the cost. The additional benefits of a small FTE reduction, significant improvements in training cycle time, increased workforce flexibility, and fewer defects in safety and quality audits further tipped the scale toward an overall reduction in costs. We had not fully anticipated the additional benefits from the improved training, so these accelerated the acceptance with less-enthusiastic managers who had been the late-adopters.

Productivity

The reduced training cycle time leads to a productivity gain equal to the difference between the two learning curves as shown in figure 11. The baseline training is indicated in the broken line and the improved training is indicated in the solid line. In this case, the gain equals two weeks of production for one FTE—the trainee. The trainer is also freed up to work more independently and regain their normal level of productivity because they no longer devote as much time to training the new trainee. These gains occur once for each new hire on a specific job or operation. A smaller gain occurs for subsequent cross-training.

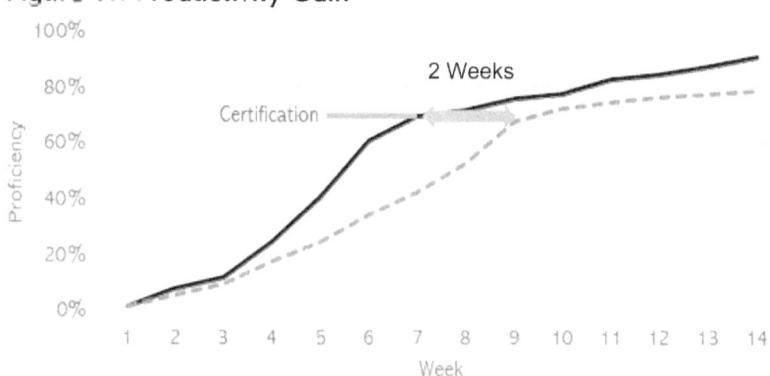

Figure 11. Productivity Gain

Additional Benefits

Additional benefits occur whenever a serious improvement effort is made in any one part of the business. Benefits gained include:

- Bringing alignment across teams, shifts, departments, and sites that are doing similar work but were using vastly different methods.

- Questions arose about the manufacturing procedures that could then be vetted out with the engineers—often leading to manufacturing process improvement and refinement.

- The new training infrastructure with Master Trainers and Training Coordinators provided a platform for enabling change. It provided a new and robust channel of communications with engineers, technology developers, management, other teams, shifts, and sites. Before this effort, it would have been extraordinary for a production team member in Burlington, Vermont to know anything about a similar operation in Corbeil-Essonnes, France or Dublin, Ireland.

- This work demonstrated the value of using principles from project management, the Capability Maturity Model, and design disciplines to define and solve problems across diverse associates and locations.

The improved process provided a continuous improvement loop needed for sustainability and which enabled further enhancement.

The Impact

For me, the most important learning from this entire experience is the impact of effective facilitating processes. It was the first instance of appreciating the role of the business process backbone. This is certainly not unique to training and is a pattern that I have continued to see throughout my work in semiconductor manufacturing, financial services, small business, non-profit, and other sectors. The effect is painfully obvious to all stakeholders, but the root causes are obscured until you take time to diligently examine the foundations upon which the value stream depends.

Sustainability

Following the process as it has been defined, continuous improvement and controls assured that it was sustained. After more than a decade, it was still in place and being constantly improved. Especially gratifying is that through both mid-level and executive-management changes, the quality of training did not unravel. Truly this was *not* failure number eleven! The MX Training Team had succeeded in meeting the original goal of instituting a sustainable training process. The experience and learning from this effort are transferrable to countless different supporting functions in both for-profit and non-profit settings including retail sales, restaurants, medical services, health sciences, transportation, call centers, administrative settings, sports, government, and charitable organizations. And it scales from small business to medium and large corporations.

The degree to which training affects overall efficiency is not an overt part of the metrics, but it clearly had a positive impact on total performance. These parallel, minimal investment impacts reinforced a sense of ownership, responsibility, and empowerment among participants as well as to increase the overall organizational value for effective training.

The real breakthrough in this entire effort is that facilitating structures are the key to making a sustainable value stream process. Simultaneously, these enable the value stream to be flexible so that it can change quickly. Then, it is through applying principles from disciplines such as the Project Management Body of Knowledge, agile philosophy, the Capability Maturity Model Integration, Quality Management, and Process Design Engineering that success can be achieved.

As I stated in chapter one, the value stream most directly impacts the customer and must be capable of changing quickly to adjust for customer, economic, market, technology, regulatory, and other conditions. Facilitating processes are mainly internal and do not have direct impact to the customer. These are generally more stable and less flexible. You will find that competitive advantage is often found in the enabling process—which is contrary to what you probably expect. I have seen proprietary designs, technology, and capabilities embedded within foundational activities. The payoff is phenomenal and extends to benefits beyond "just training" or whatever your initial focus may be.

Chapter Ten Summary

- The conclusion of our manufacturing training example
- For larger-scale efforts, test in a pilot where you can learn and adjust prior to a full-scale rollout
- Measure your progress toward the success metric and objective
- Assign clear ownership and accountability within the organization
- We met the initial objectives—and best of all, no number eleven failure!

Chapter Eleven

"She was tracking and managing all of this in a spreadsheet."

Change Management

Charlie was the executive who had built out a team of associates with expertise from various industries and finance backgrounds. Their objective—to develop and implement a customer and product profitability calculator for a large financial services enterprise. Volumes and revenues were derived from the existing lines of business systems. An activity-based costing team worked with line management to determine the drivers and costs used to calculate expenses. As each division was led through the process to define their cost drivers and then establish each cost element, a curve of adoption naturally emerged.

Early adopters became the role model to others for how to utilize the resulting insights to better manage their businesses to optimize profitability. Late adopters raised the challenging questions that had to be resolved to implement and sustain the dramatic change and cultural shift required to manage customer-level and product-level profitability. Many studies have indicated that at least 20 percent of customers are not profitable, while another 60 percent are close to break-even. The remaining customers are effectively overcharged for the products and services they buy to achieve a profit margin. An online search on this topic will provide many sources that confirm this finding.[21]

Three years into the development of the customer and product profitability calculation platform, adoption by the leadership team was beginning to take hold. As executives evaluated the monthly output showing the customer segments with their related product revenues and costs, questions naturally arose. And out of these questions, many changes were recommended. Teams began submitting various requests for change based on the monthly profitability reporting for their area. Some of the changes were well researched and ready for implementation, some were submitted as change requests, but they really amounted to challenging the data accuracy, and still others were posed as questions that could be answered from the data already being published.

An analyst named Fran said that she was tracking and managing all of these monthly requests on a spreadsheet and it was difficult to keep it updated and to provide the key stakeholders with the current version of the profitability calculations. As adoption grew across the enterprise, more lines of business were submitting changes and the spreadsheet file method was completely inadequate to manage the stream of requests. A change management process was developed and included a technology application to enable submission, implementation, testing, approval, and tracking of the change life cycle. Further, it allowed integration and regression testing of multiple changes being released into production each month.

Fran had created the spreadsheet tracking forms for the change requests. I met with her to learn the current status and ask about issues. "Fran, what is the main concern you have with your current process and forms?" Fran responded, "When we had only a few dozen requests, it worked well. But now as you can see, we have hundreds and it is hard to know which version of the spreadsheet is the current one, and I can't tell what changed from one version to the next. It is hard to track what is changing in our monthly release cycles." I wanted to know how much time it was taking Fran each week to document the new incoming change requests and then make updates to the record for progress. "Fran, how many hours a week does it take you to do all of this work?" She explained, "This is my full-time job now. My entire week is doing just this so I think there must be a better way."

We calculated the expense of the current workflow and added in the defects based on an issue log that Fran was keeping. We then met with a technology partner to estimate the cost of a simple solution that would use a SQL server database and a user interface to create, edit, and report the weekly changes. We added the expense of a project team to work on creating a process and defining the exact requirements for the technology solution. The business case indicated we would see a net positive benefit within 18 months, so it justified the improvement project.

The team referred to the Capability Maturity Model Integration Framework to guide the stakeholders through the policies, standards, high level design (process), low level design (procedures), technology, tools, and training. The low-level detail included sections for each of the knowledge areas found in The Guide to the Project Management Body of Knowledge (PMBOK).

While on one hand, the entire profitability system can be seen as a facilitating process for the financial institution, this effort was so enormous that our project team decided to look at profitability as an 'internal' value stream, and therefore, the team identified change management as a foundational process within customer and product profitability. The value stream steps included the intake of millions of transaction records from Consumer Banking, Wealth and Investment Banking, Commercial Banking, Small Business Banking, and Treasury Services. The profitability engine then used activity-based costing structures and applied these to the volumes and revenue to calculate monthly customer and product profit margins. This required change management to be robust, sustainable, and that simultaneously allows for rapid changes to flow through it to the value stream with a high assurance of successful implementation.

The customer profitability change management process supports change request submission, impact analysis, solution development, implementation, testing, and request closure. In addition, allocating the required resources, tracking, measuring results, and continuously improving the change process itself were essential. Request types include Research (to answer a specific question), Issue (fixing a problem), or Enhancement (improving the customer profitability output). The expected benefits included ability to: (1) improve communication to stakeholders to manage commitments for implementing changes, (2) reduce rework and reloads during the monthly production cycle, (3) reduce cost, and (4) reduce cycle time.

As I provide details of the change management lifecycle, the hope is that you gain value on two levels. First, that you see how investing in change management can strengthen the value stream, and second, that you might also see direct application for change management and apply it to your work.

Change Management Process

1.0 Submit request

Description: User submits a request which includes details and their contact information. The change management tracking system issues a request ID number.

2.0 Determine if request is for research

Description: Expedite research questions through a separate sub-process to do research and respond quickly.

3.0 Research question sub-process

Description: Assign a research manager to research and respond. This includes providing regular status updates to the requester and adding questions and answers to a Frequently Asked Question pool for other uses to access.

4.0 Assign request manager

Description: For requests that are not a simple question to be answered, assign a qualified request manager to oversee data analysis and to ensure a complete response is given back to the requester. The selection of the request manager is based on the scope and content of the question so that the best qualified request manager is assigned.

5.0 Perform resource impact analysis and scoping

Description: The request manager does an impact analysis, confirms the scope with the requester, and manages the work including development and testing.

6.0 Schedule request implementation

Description: In a regular meeting routine with all request managers and developers, all requests are prioritized and scheduled for a release. In agile organizations, this takes place in a scaled agile scrum-of-scrums type of routine.

7.0 Perform tasks

Description: Analysts and developers complete the work within the agreed upon schedule commitment. This work may include analysis, research, writing user stories, coding, testing, validation, and documenting the impacts for the change.

8.0 Accept test results

Description: Using a test environment and test plan, validate the solution against the request details. Document the test outcome.

9.0 Implement the solution in the production environment

Description: Implement the solution into a production release.

10.0 Accept the production results

Description: Validate that the production results meet expectations.

11.0 Close the request

Description: Close the request in the change management tracking application and ensure that all documentation and version control is updated to reflect the change in the production environment.

This workflow enabled the corporate finance team to manage changes in their monthly release cycle and to address questions and improvement requests. This rigor brought clarity and transparency to what changed from release to release and increased stakeholder confidence and satisfaction. While the change management process became stable and repeatable, it in turn allowed the profitability calculations to become more flexible without losing control of accuracy or quality.

The Increasing Rate of Change

In calculus, the derivative of a curve is the rate of change at a point on the curve. The second derivative is the rate of change of the rate of change, or stated differently, it indicates whether the rate of change itself is getting faster or not. I think that we would all agree that the second derivative of the change curve for society and economies is rapidly increasing. This quickening pace of change presents both opportunities and challenges. One of the most significant challenges is often referred to as "connecting the dots." It keeps many of us awake at night, worrying about how one change is affecting another change.

Over the past few decades, a movement toward the agile philosophy has emerged, starting with software development, and then expanding into other aspects of our business and academic environment. Overly simplified, the agile philosophy advocates for rapid cycles to learn quickly, fail early, make corrections, and be less bureaucratic. In many environments, this can lead to multiple self-directed teams all introducing change simultaneously—but not always in a fully coordinated manner. In fact, one change may conflict or cause a gap with another change. There are solutions including the scaled agile "scrum of scrums," fluid product owner routines, pre-planning sessions, and so forth. But in practice, these do not solve for the myriad of changes being developed and introduced into the real world across portfolios of scrum teams. In addition, while failing early and often leads to quicker learning, in the end, we do need to succeed!

After wrestling with this challenge and the risk of conflicting changes that it introduces across nearly every institution, I propose this facilitating process and set of tools to manage risk through better coordination. These tools are based on experience implementing them in several financial services settings, but they can apply to nearly any environment. In small-scale systems as in a small business, you may wish to implement only some of these tools and procedures to meet your needs.

Change Control Database

We created a change control database intended to reflect all known changes, including planned, in-flight, and recent changes.

This database includes the following fields for each entry:

- Name of change
- The change owner/sponsor
- Name of the process owner

- A unique identifier as a reference number for the change
- A description of the change
- The estimated project dates
- The process step(s)
- The role(s)
- The technology platform, system, application, screen, and field
- The procedure(s)
- The training
- The related laws or regulations
- The policy
- A risk rating for this change

There are several points where these changes are reviewed and compared with other changes that are either currently in flight or planned.

When a new change is proposed, there is an intake phase where we appraise the business case for the change and during the intake we should get an initial assessment for which process steps, roles, technology, procedures, training, laws, regulations, policies, and risks are affected.

As requests for change are approved, prioritized, funded, and staffed, we set an estimated timeline and can refine what we know. There is opportunity to view the impacts of the change with what is currently in flight and planned for the near term. There will be tollgates, showcases, scrum reviews or other similar updates for the work in progress. Here, we can utilize the scrum of scrums or stakeholder reviews to examine how this change fits with other known changes.

The change will be tested to see if it performs as expected. This should include conducting a regression test to ensure that the change fits with the known environment.

After a final review and acceptance by the change sponsor, it is documented. Training is completed and then the change is fully implemented into the production environment.

The data base of changes and impacts must be maintained by an owner who attends the change reviews across the various initiatives and makes the necessary information updates. This may be delegated to project or scrum teams to update, but at critical points there will be reviews of all known changes and the owner of this central change control database plays a key role to ensure that conflicts, overlaps, gaps, and issues are raised and resolved.

The resolution path itself becomes a work stream with actions, owners, and dates to resolve the identified conflicts, gaps, and issues. The follow-up timing can be included in the stakeholder or showcase reviews.

Figure 12 shows a template for tracking changes aligned to strategic goals, process steps, and the scrum teams delivering the change.

Figure 12. Inventory of Process Change

Value Stream Process	Level 2 Process	Level 3 Process	Strategic Goal	Scrum 1 Deliverable	Scrum 2 Deliverable	Scrum 3 Deliverable
1.0	1.1	1.1.1				
		1.1.2				
		1.1.3				
	1.2	1.2.1				
		1.2.2				
	1.3	1.3.1				
2.0	2.1	2.1.1				
		2.1.2				
		2.1.3				
	2.2	2.2.1				
		2.2.2				

For each change, this record is created and then maintained. Figure 13 shows a list of fields—and more could be added based on your specific needs. Ideally, this is linked to trusted data sources so that the data is always current. To illustrate, linkage to the procedures would connect the user directly to a data base with the current version. Even if linkage to the source is not available, at a minimum, the reference should state which document or data needs to be reviewed and where to locate it.

Figure 13. Data Elements in a Change Record

- Request Title
- Requester
- Requester Contact Information
- Sponsor
- Purpose for the Request
- Description
- Date Required for Implementation
- Alignment to Strategic Goal
- Value Stream Process Step
- Level 2 Process
- Level 3 Process
- Policy
- Role
- Technology Platform
- Technology Application
- Technology Screen and Field
- Procedure
- Training
- Law
- Regulation
- Metric
- Scrum Team
- Release Timing

A user could query this data base for a specific process step, procedure, technology, or other attribute to get a report on all in-flight or planned changes that might affect that element. From there, the user can contact the impacted owners to conduct stakeholder analysis and consultation. Each team working on the same element should all be aware of each other's work so that they can coordinate an integrated solution.

Change Integration Management

Although there are established change control processes to manage versions, often there is a gap in tracking all changes in relation to each other. Throughout the life cycle of the project or scrum, changes can be continually evaluated for impacts to other in-flight or planned changes. The release timing plays a key role in understanding cross-project impacts and interdependencies.

In the book titled *Orchestrating Transformation: How to Deliver Winning Performance with a Connected Approach to Change* (2019),[22] authors Michael Wade, James Macaulay, Andy Noronha, and Joel Barbier describe three types of interdependence. They are sequential, pooled, and reciprocal.

Sequential is described as a series of tasks where the output of each step becomes the input to the next one. A demonstration of sequential interdependence is an assembly line operation.

Pooled interdependence is where the independent and parallel outputs of steps all contribute to the final output. Each individual function or sub-process does not rely on another one, but the final output is from the combination of all independent sub-processes. A way to think about pooled interdependence is a group of parallel activities that can happen in any order or sequence without impacting each other, but the final output requires all to be completed. To illustrate, a loan application requires income, asset, liability, and collateral information which can arrive independently, but all the information must be available before the underwriter can determine whether to approve the application.

The third type of interdependence is reciprocal. Here the steps may all interact with exchanges of inputs and outputs between them to make a final output. Development of a technology solution has reciprocal interdependence where several software modules must be simultaneously created with ongoing exchanges between the agile scrum teams to ensure that the modules work together as an integrated and effective solution.

Combinations of the three types of interdependencies are likely to exist in more complex environments.

The increasing pace of change and the complexity of interdependence makes change integration management more critical to mitigating the risk of conflicts and gaps. To manage across multiple and simultaneous changes and with various types and combinations of interdependence requires a multi-dimensional change management approach.

Based on the attributes above, this multi-dimensional approach should:

- Create a change record for all changes
- Establish an owner or sponsor for each change
- Review each proposed change in a regular forum of stakeholders (e.g., you could conduct a weekly change integration management meeting where these new changes are presented by the change sponsor or delegate and reviewed by key stakeholders and product owners)
- Ensure that all change data elements are also being managed and updated by their respective owners (e.g., process, procedures, training, policy)
- Implement version control

As conflicts and gaps are discovered, assign an owner and a target resolution date. The resolution to conflicts and gaps become additional change that must be managed and should be represented in the Change Control Database.

This effort is significant, so it may be necessary to start small with creating the change management database and entering changes for just two portfolios of change from related groups of scrum teams or project teams that have known interdependencies. The basic routines could be established for stakeholder reviews and refined based on experience. As the routines begin to become effective, additional portfolios of change could be added and the known web of interdependencies would naturally grow. The intent is to mitigate the risk of conflicts and gaps as multiple changes are planned, in flight, tested, and implemented.

Benefits of Change Management

Comprehensive change management process improvement led to the desired flexibility in addressing changes while ensuring version management and control. The cost of development and implementation was offset by a reduction in staffing that we previously required to manually track changes, and less rework due to errors. Balancing flexibility with stability may be more evident in change management than any other activity.

Change management is common across all organizations and is a critical facilitating process that supports the value stream. Whether you implement change management with a database like what I have described, or choose to solve this in some other way, it is a process that merits serious investment. If changes are not effectively managed and controlled, you will disrupt your value stream and risk a detrimental effect on your customers.

Chapter Eleven Summary

- Virtually all value stream processes require some type of change management process

- As a demonstration of recursive or 'nested' processes, the corporate profitability platform is a facilitating process in the financial management of a large enterprise and within it, there is another level of enabling process for managing change

- A change management process model is provided which you may find useful

- Change integration management is highlighted as a need for controlling multiple, simultaneous changes

Chapter Twelve

"If they fail, they can have significant impact."

Additional Examples

Like the executives in the manufacturing training example, if you have failed at implementing and sustaining change ten times before, assess the facilitating processes within your own work. You may well find that the root-cause of failure exists there. These are also your most effective risk management and control functions, and where you can create competitive advantage. Let us now see how you can apply this learning to other situations. First, I want to explain that I am describing some possible applications which are based on my experience from manufacturing and financial services, but I have not personally analyzed nor implemented change in these business sectors. These are not intended to be definitive. They are for illustrative purposes only and intended for you to see how we could apply the concept of value stream and foundational designs.

Health Care

Value Stream

Let us look at a hospital and first think about the value stream process. The activities that directly touch the patient include scheduling the visit, admitting the patient, conducting an examination of vital signs, reviewing the patient's medical history and current health condition, administering diagnostic testing, completing medical procedures, providing recovery and nursing care, and releasing the patient from the facility.

Facilitating

To support these activities, you can imagine facilitating processes such as scheduling operating rooms, scheduling medical staff, managing the supply chain of equipment and supplies, testing blood samples, managing the housekeeping staff, managing the facilities systems, providing food services, and directing the hospital finance team. While the patient may never meet the people doing some of these tasks, they are all essential to the medical facility and to enable patient care and services. You can also see that although many of the tasks are done behind the scenes, if they fail, they can have significant impact to the patient experience. Potential failures include delayed admission, inability to complete required testing, giving the patient an incorrect medicine or treatment, not maintaining a clean and safe patient environment, and inaccurate billing for services.

Technology

Technology often enables an enterprise. Because technology can be substantial as both an infrastructure and as an organization, if we treat technology as a value stream, then within technology development there are also facilitating processes. A state within the United States implemented toll roads and utilized technology solutions that can either sense a transponder on a vehicle taking the toll road, or the system can take a photo of the state vehicle registration tag and send a toll bill to the registered owner of the vehicle. If the transponder is sensed, an account set up by the vehicle owner is directly charged for the toll rate.

Value Stream

The value stream for the vehicle driver in this case is that they use the toll road, and the vehicle owner gets directly billed for the toll. The value stream for the state is that they collect revenue from vehicles using the toll road.

Facilitating

First, the hardware includes the overhead structure with cameras and sensors on the toll highway, transponders attached to the vehicle windshields, the toll system processor and memory, the network used to route data from the sensors and cameras to the server and host hardware. The architectural design and management of this entire hardware platform could be a facilitating process. Failure or defects in the network or devices cause disruption to the value stream applications and services. However, most of us do not experience frequent failure in the hardware or network because this has been managed to become resilient and reliable to avoid these disruptions. Investment to make these supporting processes and the related infrastructure stable, in turn, enables the value stream to remain in operation and to be flexible to meet customer needs.

Second, the software includes the state department of transportation web site where vehicle owners can establish an account and order a transponder. The online application takes vehicle identity information and bills the vehicle owner. Additionally, customer user-story definition, development techniques, scrum management, information security, testing, and quality control are all enabling processes.

Cases of information breaches are all too common. While the technology solution (value stream) may work well for the main customer need, protecting the information and keeping it secure from data breaches (facilitating) is at least as critical, and may be seen as a competitive advantage for sensitive personal, corporate, or government information. Significant investment in data security will likely pay off as customers and clients understand the rigor used to protect their information. Conversely, customers who may enjoy and appreciate the value stream services may be driven away from your technology if they learn that it is vulnerable to hacking and breaches. In some cases, you may even be liable for the losses and related risks to your customers.

Project Management

In the introduction, I included reference to the Project Management Institute (PMI) and their Guide to the Project Management Body of Knowledge (PMBOK). This guide includes ten knowledge areas in the Sixth Edition published by PMI in 2017.[23] These knowledge areas are:

- Project Integration Management
- Project Scope Management
- Project Schedule Management
- Project Cost Management
- Project Quality Management
- Project Resource Management
- Project Communications Management
- Project Risk Management
- Project Procurement Management
- Project Stakeholder Management

The entire project management lifecycle is a critical facilitating process for most organizations. Whether it is in the form of agile, predictive/waterfall, iterative, or incremental—project management is a way of managing change and change is ubiquitous. As we saw in several other case studies, this project/change process is large enough to be separated into value stream (delivering change) and facilitating (managing and controlling the development and implementation of the change) components. The health care sector scenario described above requires managing the patient experience at a hospital. If you need to improve patient scheduling, you might focus on access for patients, other medical offices, and the hospital admitting team to view online scheduling options.

Value Stream

The value stream of the project is delivering the desired improvement in the scheduling capability to benefit the patient experience, allowing the customer (patient) to select from available scheduling options through an online application.

Facilitating

In project management, enabling processes may include activities for planning scrum team daily stand ups, updating the scrum team sprint board, organizational planning, quality planning, and scheduling scrum-of-scrums routines.

Topics such as schedule management, cost management, quality management, and resource management could support many other value stream steps. These stable processes then allow the organization to deliver change, keep the value stream flexible, meet customer demands, adapt to macro-environmental changes, and to innovate.

In the hospital scheduling improvement, ensure that the entire life cycle of change is managed with high quality for a great customer/patient experience that simultaneously works effectively for the hospital.

I recommend further study of the project management processes and knowledge areas to better understand the nature of facilitating functions.

Communication

For this sector, I will use the telecommunications industry. Mobile communications is a value stream that delivers data and information to end users, and it is also a facilitating process for an organization doing some other business such as health care, financial services, manufacturing, retail sales, or transportation.

Value Stream

The user needs the value stream to carry data and voice reliably and securely from one point to another point and to provide personal data storage and access.

Facilitating

There is physical infrastructure of cell towers, diplexers, antennas, routers, satellites, data storage centers, devices, and accessories. On another level, there are processes to manage the supply chain, sales, billing, the mobile phone operating systems, agreements with mobile device manufacturers, and other carriers. Third party providers are essential for the development of user apps that drive more telecommunications demand. By looking at failure modes in the value stream process, the telecommunications service provider can identify the most critical business backbone components and invest heavily to make them stable and reliable.

Transportation

When you place an online order, you expect quick delivery with no damage to your item. The network of transporting and tracking your product from a manufacturer to a warehouse and then to your door is extensive and complex. Yet, to you as a customer, it must seem nearly transparent. You place your order and wait for the doorbell to ring.

Value Stream

There could be a series of forklifts, trucks, conveyor belts, and people moving your item along the delivery path. There is also a method for tracking the progress so that you can check on the status and location at any time. You have an expectation for when it will be delivered, and in many cases, there is a committed time window for arrival, and all at little to no cost. This is the value stream as perceived by the customer.

Facilitating

Extensive infrastructure of vehicles, buildings, storage, and tracking are integral elements. Staffing and scheduling, sorting, routing, tracking and status reporting, damage prevention, security, and many other processes are required.

Transportation is one of the greatest examples where complex enabling systems can make the value stream appear simple. Having your package delivered on time, flying across your country, using a ride share service, and expecting your local grocery store to be completely stocked require extensive work to occur based on stable and reliable facilitating processes. Those transportation providers who make it look the simplest are often the competitive winners. Those providers have invested the most in design, managing the details, ensuring back up plans are in place, and measuring their performance.

Data

It is unfathomable to comprehend the amount of data collected and stored across the world every second. This data is used for virtually all aspects of our lives.

Value Stream

In the transportation case described above, an online retailer relies on sourcing and then selling you goods and services. A data value stream could exist for the tracking of the goods along the entire end-to-end workflow from manufacturer to you as a final customer. This would include the item description, inventory, availability, location, cost, pricing, customer feedback, and product ratings. You as a consumer of the product or service are a customer, and the retailer is a customer of the data value stream process. Each of these customers has different but overlapping interests in the data.

Facilitating

Most likely there will be several separate but interconnected systems involved in the data value stream. The manufacturer will have a production tracking application and a sales system, the online retailer will have purchasing, inventory, sales, and distribution technology, and the transportation provider will have scheduling, routing, and tracking capability. Each requires a set of data processes and resources which are reliable to support the value stream.

The benefit of having the data includes ability to manage and analyze performance. Both rely on accurate data—so once again we see the critical nature of the facilitating processes.

Chapter Twelve Summary

- Use these descriptions from various industries and applications to envision how you would define your own value stream and facilitating operations

Chapter Thirteen

"What is your No Number Eleven?"

Strengthen Your Business Process Backbone

Let us take a moment to refresh the definitions given in the introduction.

CORE or VALUE STREAM process: Key activity or cluster of activities which must be performed in an exemplary manner to ensure a firm's continued competitiveness because it adds primary value to an output.

FACILITATING process: An activity or cluster of activities that do not of themselves add primary value to a customer or end-user output but are performed internally by the organization to support and make it possible to accomplish the core processes. These enabling functions often relate to multiple value stream steps.

Practitioners who attempt to build a robust business using methods such as project management, process design, and concepts from the Capability Maturity Model face the challenge of multi-month if not multi-year efforts during which time they are likely to experience intense and rapid internal and external changes. By separating the workflow into value stream (customer facing) and facilitating (internal), we use an approach that produces a highly flexible value stream and a stable, robust, and sustainable foundation.

Small Business and Less Complex Operations

When applying these concepts in a small business or less complex operation, on one hand, you will have fewer resources and less time to commit to analysis and design. On the other hand, you may benefit from even a modest investment in understanding and improving supporting processes that are causing issues in your value stream.

- You can use an "and" approach by adding improvement efforts within your current activities and interactions.

- Use a lighter version of the methods shared in this book as they apply to you. One or two key enhancements may make a positive difference.

- Discuss this topic of conversation as you interact with other entrepreneurs to share the awareness and possible solutions.

- You can benchmark with small business owners as you offer to compare practices and conduct a review for each other. You may gain the most value by partnering with a venture which is different than yours.

- Look at the list later in this chapter and determine your critical foundational functions. This is not a comprehensive list, but it may prompt you to think through yours. Do any of these relate to the challenges that you currently face, or risks and opportunities that you identified in your assessment?

- When you have time and resources to invest, determine if one of your facilitating processes will bring you the most benefit.

What Is Your No Number Eleven?

In the manufacturing training case, executives complained of failing ten times before and asked how this time would be different. The team commissioned to tackle the problem adopted the mantra of "No Number Eleven" failure. The success of that effort became a watermark in my career. I learned about the importance of foundational, internal functions and the balance between them and the customer-facing work. I also learned that significant investment in the business process backbone pays off when focused on the right failures and opportunities. Since then, I have been advising executives and managers and have found favorable acknowledgement. They resonate with managers who face challenges similar to those that I have shared. They readily admit making decisions that put large scale efforts suddenly on hold, disbanding teams, and wasting months or years of effort. They also recognize that there is a simultaneous need for both stability and flexibility. An appreciation of value stream and facilitating activities reconciles the dissonance in two opposing forces. Are you facing this opposition? Do the stories in this book resonate with you as well? If so, I invite you to join with me in applying and testing this theory to see if we can find further success in its application.

This is our recommended approach:

1. Write out your value stream flow.

    Think about starting with your customer and ending with your customer and list the steps where your customer sees value.

2. Write out your backbone or enabling activities.

    List the other work that you do which is not visible to your customer—internal operations and functions. Consider that some may be missing.

3. Assess the value of each activity. You can use three ratings; customer value-add, internal business value-add, non-value add which is wasteful effort.

4. Conduct root-cause analysis as a reactive method.

    For known failure modes, you can use a root-cause analysis method to find why defects occur.

5. Complete a risk and opportunity assessment as a proactive method.

   The most effective technique is to intentionally design facilitating processes to achieve the strongest possible value-add.

6. Prioritize the most critical ones for investment to create your competitive and proprietary advantage.

   Define your primary objectives, success metrics, defects, risks, and innovative opportunities. Rate these and use the rating to identify the most critical area to improve.

7. Design the backbone functions.

   Use the structure of common features and operational framework shared in chapter three.

8. Pilot and test.
9. Use the initial outcome and learning to refine.
10. Implement and measure your results.

The root cause analysis and the proactive risk and opportunity assessment are critical success factors in this entire effort. When you determine where your significant failure modes and innovative opportunities exist, you may find they are in the value stream, but be sure to also evaluate facilitating processes such as these:

- Business Continuity Planning for natural and human-made disruption
- Change Management
- Compliance Management
- Facilities Management
- Finance Management
    - Profit and Loss Accounting
    - Budgeting for Change Initiatives

- Human Resource Management
    - Capacity Planning
    - Performance Management
    - Recruiting
    - Training Management
- Infrastructure Management
    - Applications
    - Database
    - Distribution and Delivery
    - Inventory Storage
    - Network
    - Technology Platform
- Legal Processes
- Marketing and Customer Acquisition
- Policy Formulation
- Quality Management
- Risk Management
- Supply Chain Management

What have you failed at ten times before and need to finally address with certainty? What is going to be your No Number Eleven? Does your business process backbone need to be strengthened? If you are experiencing a persistent failure mode and have not yet been able to sustain a solution, it is likely to be a failure mode in a facilitating process. Or you may be facing competition that is taking some of your business and you need to find your superior edge. Applying significant rigor can lead to a sustainable solution and could also become a competitive advantage. As with the experience of our financial services, manufacturing, and small business teams, I believe that you can have significant success. Most organizations will not commit to this kind of work, but this is worth substantial investment. Some solutions may even lead to proprietary designs and become your competitive advantage, turning a failure mode into a strength!

Notes

1. A Guide to The Project Management Body of Knowledge, Project Management Institute, Newtown Square, Pennsylvania, USA. See www.pmi.org.

2. The Capability Maturity Model Integration, Carnegie Innovations, Pittsburgh, Pennsylvania, USA. See www.cmmiinstitute.com.

3. Quality Management and Process Design are fact-driven, disciplined approaches to eliminating waste, reducing defects, and improving quality. References include www.isixsigma.com and www.asq.com.

4. See "core process" at www.businessdictionary.com.

5. Dauphinee, J. (2020). Definition of facilitating process offered by the author.

6. "Keystone species and conserving our delicate food web" presented by Agnes Mittermayr, https://www.youtube.com/watch?v=0he3ApJVS50.

7. The Innovator's Dilemma: When New Technologies Cause Great Firms to Fail, Clayton M. Christensen, Harvard Business Review Press, Boston, Massachusetts, 1997, 2000, 2016.

8. The 8th Habit: From Effectiveness to Greatness, Stephen R. Covey, Free Press, New York, 2005.

9. what's your problem?, Thomas Wedell-Wedellsborg, Harvard Business Review Press, Boston, Massachusetts, 2020.

10. According to the author's research, the statement "it is direction first, then velocity" originates from a religious address given by Neal A. Maxwell in October 1976. See https://www.churchofjesuschrist.org/study/general-conference/1976/10/notwithstanding-my-weakness?lang=eng.

11. For a references to moving from one maturity level to another, see www.cmmiinstitute.com.

12. The Principles of Scientific Management, Frederick Winslow Taylor, Harper & Brothers Publishers, New York, New York 1919.

13. "Passport to Leadership," BYU Magazine, Brigham Young University, Provo, Utah, Fall 2013, Volume 67, Number 4.

14. For a description of lean agile scrum, see www.asq.org.

15. Discover Card Commercial ("Peggy—Support"), 2010, https://www.youtube.com/watch?v=xpDEMThc5fw&list=PLFVt6LGoIqmSO2qlfSoEwUajrooDU214-.

16. Artificial intelligence is defined as the study of intelligent agents in Computational Intelligence—A Logical Approach, Poole, Mackworth, and Goebel, Oxford University Press, New York, New York, 1998.

17. Application Programming Interface is software that allows various technology applications to communicate with each other.

18. Flight to quality is a phrase used to describe when investors move from a high risk to a lower risk investment option. In this specific reference, I am applying the phrase to consumers and small business owners who moved their banking accounts to institutions perceived to be safer and more trustworthy during the U.S. economic recession of 2009. Similar moves were made by investors in 2020 due to the economic impact of the Covid-19 pandemic.

19. Development and Implementation of a Sustainable Operator Training and Certification Process, Jeffrey L. Dauphinee, 2001, IEEE Symposium on Semiconductor Manufacturing, Cat. No. 01CH37203, see https://ieeexplore.ieee.org/abstract/document/963026.

20. For a description of process maturity levels, see www.cmmiinstitute.com.

21. To see a brief explanation of customer profitability, see https://www2.deloitte.com/us/en/insights/deloitte-review/issue-5/how-profitable-are-your-customers-really.html.

22. Orchestrating Transformation: How to Deliver Winning Performance with a Connected Approach to Change, Michael Wade, James Macaulay, Andy Noronha, and Joel Barbier, International Institute for Management Development, Lausanne, Switzerland, 2019.

23. A Guide to the Project Management Body of Knowledge, PMBOK Guide, Sixth Edition, Project Management Institute, Newtown Square, Pennsylvania, 2017.

Index

agile philosophy, 17, 101
agile scrum, 26, 41
agile scrum of scrums, 99
amphipods, 11
backbone business process definition, 6
Barbier, Joel, 105
call center, 41
Capability Maturity Model Integration (CMMI), 30
change control database, 101
change integration management, 105
change management, 95
Christensen, Clayton, 16
common features, 31
competitive advantage, 29, 94
Covey, Stephen R., 17
facilitating process definition, 6
Guide to the Project Management Body of Knowledge (PMBOK), 5, 112
Macauley, James, 105
keystone species, 11
lean agile scrum, 41

mortgage process, 21
Noronha, Andy, 105
operational framework, 31
plan, do, check, act, 31
process maturity, 36, 63
profitability, 95
Project Management Institute (PMI), 5, 112
proprietary, 29
residential flooring, 53
risk assessment, 56
root-cause, 25
small business, 47, 53, 118
small business banker, 47
Taylor, Frederick Winslow, 36
training process, 59
transformational change, 36
value stream process definition, 6
Wade, Michael, 105
Weddell-Weddellsborg, Thomas, 26
Weidman, David N., 36
whitewater, 17

Acknowledgments

I gratefully extend my sincere appreciation to many whom I know and many others whom I have never met but who have influenced my work and my life. The most prominent of those I know is Alan Vercio, my former manager. Alan became a friend, a mentor, and a coach to me and saw capability in myself that I did not yet see. He encouraged, challenged, and taught me. He was instrumental in the discovery of how facilitating processes function.

Other influencers include Joel Barbier, the Capability Maturity Model Integration Institute, Clayton M. Christensen, Stephen R. Covey, James Macaulay, Neal A. Maxwell, Andy Noronha, the Project Management Institute, Frederick Winslow Taylor, Michael Wade, Thomas Wedell-Wedellsborg, and David N. Weidman.

About the Author

Jeffrey L. Dauphinee is a certified Project Management Professional® and Six Sigma Master Black Belt. He has led teams of manufacturing engineers and technicians, process engineering managers, process design engineers, and process owners in manufacturing, engineering, and financial services. He has authored and co-authored articles and whitepapers published in the Project Management Institute Knowledge Shelf, Journal of Corporate Accounting & Finance (Wiley Publications) and presented at Sematech semiconductor consortium and Institute of Electrical and Electronic Engineers symposia. *Strengthen Your Business Process Backbone: The Unappreciated Value of Facilitating Processes* is his first published book.

www.ingramcontent.com/pod-product-compliance
Lightning Source LLC
Chambersburg PA
CBHW020431220526
45464CB00002B/655